Mama's Story

Of Love and Hope

BY HAZEL LEE PINKSTON

Mama's Story of Love and Hope

Printed in the USA by Morris Publishing®

P.O. Box 2110, 3212 E. Hwy. 30

Kearney, NE 68848-2110

800-650-7888

www.morrispublishing.com

ISBN: 978-0-578-36334-9

DEDICATION

For my children,

grandchildren

and great grandchildren.

In the hope

that through the writing of this book,

you all will have a better understanding,

and know more about

the character and rugged way of life

of your parents, grandparents, and great
grandparents.

Hazel Lee Pinkston

(Mother, Mama, Granny)

*These commandments that I give you today are to
be upon your hearts. Impress them on your children.
Deuteronomy 6:6-7*

TABLE OF CONTENTS

INTRODUCTION

It is with great honor that I have the opportunity to write this because I knew the author, my mama, Hazel Lee Pinkston.

Years ago, Mama began collecting pieces of history and recording events that happened during her childhood and beyond. Mama didn't get to finish high school but was the smartest person I knew. She taught herself to do anything she set out to do, whether it was sewing, building, or driving. Daddy, Cecil Pinkston, used to say she wasn't afraid of the devil, and she wasn't, but she was afraid of bad weather.

In this book, you will read about history, about how everyone lived during hard times and how they survived. Mama's faith and love of God, family and others is what kept her going in very difficult times.

This book is a story about a young lady and a gentle man, as Mama called Daddy, who fell in love, married, had a family, and how Mama survived a tragedy.

We hope through the writings of this book, that whatever situation you may find yourself in, that you find hope through Mama's faith.

Linda Pinkston Dalton

ACKNOWLEDGEMENTS

First of all, we'd like to give thanks to our Creator and Sustainer. We are eternally grateful to have been born into our family. No matter the circumstances we were in, our Daddy and Mama, Cecil Pinkston and Hazel Lee Pinkston, always taught us to be thankful, to love God and each other, to work hard, to be honest and give to others who might not have as much as we had.

We'd like to acknowledge our paternal grandparents, Lester and Mary Pinkston, also known as Pinky Ma and Pinky Pa, who we were fortunate enough to grow up next door to. We learned so much from them and spent hours listening to them tell stories that we still tell today.

We'd also like to acknowledge our maternal grandparents, Robert and Lillie Lee, also known as Pa and Ma Lee, who were the epitome of true examples, teaching us what family is about. Their love, devotion, and loyalty will always live on in each one of us.

Our mama wrote this book years ago in hopes her children and grandchildren, and those yet to come, would get a glimpse into hardships they faced, overcoming adversity, sickness and death, and happy times families shared when life was simpler, but also much harder. We are forever thankful that Mama wrote this, not only for us, but for us to share with the world.

For my siblings, I give thanks to God always for each of you. My sister, Mary Pinkston Luman, is the best sister ever, and I couldn't have ever asked for brothers any better than Charles Pinkston and Edward Pinkston. We have always stood together in good times and bad.

A special thanks to Mindy Stanley, Mama and Daddy's great granddaughter, for designing the front and back book cover.

A special thanks to Karen Lee Thomas, Mama's niece, who spent many hours typing this manuscript, as well as researching when questions arose.

We are also very thankful for the platform we've been blessed to have on social media, Facebook – Pinky Ma's Cakes, Cookies & Candy (Sisters in the Kitchen), You Tube – PinkyMa's Kitchen, and last but not least, our faithful friends, followers, and viewers on social media.

HAZEL LEE PINKSTON

CECIL R. PINKSTON

PRECIOUS MEMORIES OF MY MOM AND DAD

One looks backward, and one looks forward. One is of today and the other for tomorrow.

Memory is history recorded in our brain. Memory can also be likened to a painter. They paint pictures of the past and of the present. It's not until one looks back on their past that they realize the reality of oneself, and their view of things as a child.

Children can and do realize what is going on around them and have quite good judgements of events and people. This means if things are going well, a child is happy, but when Mom and Dad are angry with each other, a child will be sad and remember it long hours to come.

I am thankful to say that my parents gave me a great sense of security and happiness. Mom and Dad did not argue or quarrel at all. If they did, we did not know it. I must have been about ten or twelve years of age when I really began to understand that there was not nothing in the world which was so venerable as the character of my parents. They were to be worthy of reverence by me at this time in my life, and even much more so, as they grew older. Nothing so tender as that of parents and their children. Dad and Mom loved their children, grandchildren, and great grandchildren.

I'm thankful to have had a loving relationship with my brothers and sisters. They have all been so very good to me so many times.

I loved to wake up in the morning hearing Dad and Mom in the kitchen, talking to each other. Then, every once in a while, talking to the baby. You see the baby always gets up when Mom and Dad does. Perhaps Mom had already been to the cow pen and milked the cow. Dad did the field work from daybreak until dark, but he didn't cater much to milking, unless he had to. Elsie learned to milk and helped Mom. I was too afraid of a cow to learn to milk.

ROBERT DANIEL LEE

Robert Daniel Lee was my father. 'Pa' Lee was born on November 21, 1903. He was married to Lillie Lorene Hooper on November 22, 1924.

DAD DISOBEYING HIS MAMA

When Dad was a boy, they had a peach orchard and Dad loved to climb the trees. Grandma had told him many times, "Robert, don't climb those peach trees anymore!" He did not obey her, and he fell out of the tree and cut his leg very, very badly. I know this, not only because he told us, but we saw that bad scar on that leg as long as he lived. It must have literally taken all the flesh off that particular part that was cut because of the way it looked, only the skin was at that place.

MY DAD'S PERSONALITY

My dad had a bad temper before receiving the Holy Ghost. I don't mean that he was quick to be angered, but I have seen him get angry when he thought someone was being wronged, even if it wasn't him. God really changed that in him.

My dad loved his wife and children, also his mom and dad, his sisters, and brothers. He just loved to visit his relatives and friends. Dad was a man of his word.

I remember when his mama, my Grandmother Lee, was sick. We children didn't realize how badly ill she was. Dad had been to town and bought Grandmother fruit juices, ice cream, etc. Hershel asked dad why he didn't buy any for us. I remember distinctly Dad telling him that "Grandmother was very sick." And he replied, "If it takes the shirt off my back, I'll do everything and anything to help her."

4

Grandmother Lee did pass away not long after this on May 4th, 1935. She had cancer.

DAD WAS A HARD WORKER

One of the most fortunate things in life that can happen to us is to have a happy childhood. Looking back, I think Mom and Dad for the most part was agreeable with each other. Nowadays people don't stress the fact of being agreeable. When one is agreeable, he most likely has lots of friends and acquaintances. My Dad was that kind of person. Nowadays, people tend to ask, "if a man has a good job?", "what about his education?" or "what he's contributing to society?". Dad only had a grammar school education, but he had great hopes, purposes, and he resolved to make a good living and provide for his household, and he did. He worked from sunup to sundown and many times thru the night. He was willing to devote himself to the toilsome work which he seemed to understand was the price of being a success.

Dad worked as a farmer, usually as a sharecropper. This meant they gave the person who owned the land a portion of what they made, not necessarily a portion of what was raised but rather a portion of the money, derived from crops.

After crops were gathered, Dad always had an old pick-up or hoopie we called them, later he was able to purchase a large truck. Anyway, he went away from home and bought produce and sold it for profit. This helped supplement his income.

I speak of Pa Lee when I say Dad. He was a trader, buyer, seller of anything to make money that was right in God's sight.

Dad was a grocery peddler for several years. He had an old van, and he went all over the county, stopping from house to house selling groceries, sometimes he let me go with him.

Dad was a hardworking man. He would get up early and leave the house, go to the fields, cut bushes, burn brush, disc the land, prepare the soil, all in preparation of spring planting. The work of planting meant long hours in the hot, dusty fields.

In the early years of my school days, they had some government projects which men in the community worked on. It was called W.P.A. Dad worked on this road project.

Then they started a school lunch program for the school children to eat lunch at Mrs. Pearl Taylor's home. We kids thought that was a great and grand idea, but you would have thought we had been singled out for us and us alone. Mom finally persuaded Dad to let us eat there, I don't believe we ate there but about 1 month or 2 at the most.

One thing Dad did was a real fearful thing for me, also Mom. Dad literally loved to break a wild horse. He built a splendid tall plank fence around his breaking lot and many Sundays all his friends came over to ride the wild horses. I was so afraid Dad would get killed.

In the year of 1937 and 1938, my dad would go squirrel hunting every few days and come back with a sack full. Since there were lots of hickory nuts and things for the squirrels to feed upon, they were very fat and, my, such good meat. This sure helped to put something different in the way of meat on our table. Mom made squirrel dumplings and fried squirrel and gravy. It was delicious.

When Dad left the defense work at Freeport, TX, he came back to East Texas to buy the farm at the Attoyac River. This was not the first place that Dad owned but it was to be his home for the next 38 years, until his death. He bought this farm in 1942.

Later years Dad had a mechanic shop. He was a good mechanic. He solicited my help many times. I often think that God was preparing me for the many years I'd be on my own and the things I learned then has been useful for me now.

Then when the war came, Dad went to the defense plants and worked. Also, Dad worked in the concrete foundation business some with my Uncle Covy. He also was a pretty good carpenter. He did lots of work around the community, building rooms, roofs, and repair work.

Then Dad bought dairy cows, horses, farming equipment, hogs, chickens, you name it. He soon built a dairy barn and ran that for many years. Mom and perhaps some of the other children helped to run and operate it. I was married by then.

LILLIE LORENE HOOPER LEE (MA)

Lillie Lorene Hooper Lee was my mother. 'Ma' Lee was born March 7, 1903. She was very smart in school, and from all accounts, she had a great love for art and poetry. She married my dad, Robert Daniel Lee, on November 22, 1924.

MY MEMORIES OF MOM

My first memories of my mom, Ma Lee, was at a very early age 2 ½ or 3 years of age. Mom was a person, as I saw it, hard to get acquainted with. I think perhaps due to the fact that she had so many children, she did not have time to visit, especially wasting any of her valuable time. I'm quite sure that this was instilled in me, some of these traits.

Mom was a person whose worth could only be estimated by the real goodness of her heart. Overall, I think Mom had a well-balanced temper. Dad had a terrible temper until God filled him with the Holy Ghost. Mom was a trustworthy person. I heard my dad say one time, "He would not live with a woman he could not trust." He was not saying this to be disrespectful. He said it as an honor to her.

Mom was truthful in all things, never exaggerated things. She believed that if she had respect and affection, the outcome would be confidence. I think she was right. This made her have influence upon Dad, as well as her children, neighbors, and family. We cannot live without having some sort of influence. We need to be aware as to what kind of influence we are constantly passing on to others. Is it good or bad?

I was interested in my parents, because they were my parents, also because they achieved that very rare production: a happy marriage. This proved to me that with all the trials of life, if they made it, I could too. Without trials, we can't guess at our own strength. Hardships are the soil of manhood and self-reliance.

The Bible speaks much in Proverbs 31:10-26 about a good woman. How she works, tends to her own household, and therefore makes her husband trust in her, and scripture says, makes her price more valuable than rubies.

Most everyone who knew Mom would agree that she spent most of her time in her kitchen. Mom worked consistently but she was slow. She also did her cooking with great care. She could make the plainest dishes taste like a king's meal.

I remember going home for lunch from the fields, not knowing what was for lunch, but always knowing it would be delicious and plentiful. Mom hardly ever sat down at the table to eat with us, she waited the table.

As a young lady, Mom was a very good artist and a good student. She had lots of her report cards. She made A+++ on many papers. Then, after finishing all grades at Excelsior, she filled in as a substitute teacher.

Then she and Aunt Pearl run a telephone switchboard at Aiken. She was working there the day World War I ended, got the calls on the telephone about the war being over. They heard everyone going out and shooting guns in the air.

Mom saw the first car to come thru Aiken, scared all the horses nearly to death. Mom also saw the first and last Haley's Comet in the sky.

GIFT OF LOVE

Mom told me all along that she was going to give me a pretty mink stole that she had. She'd get it out and show me every now and then. This was for her appreciation of my helping her. She did give it to me. It burned up in our house fire, in 1951 after I married.

BIRTHDAYS

Mom tried to do something special for Hershel and my birthdays up until about 6 years of age. Usually, it was a watermelon feast or ice cream.

MOM WAS A REAL HOMEMAKER

Mom was a good wife, good mother, and kind and devoted to Dad and her children.

Dad never expected Mom to work in the field. She had a garden and tended it with great care and pride. Dad prepared the garden, plowing and rowing up the rows, planting the Irish potatoes and then turning it over to Mom.

Mom was a real homemaker. She not only had 14 children, but she did all the things that go with child raising. Remember there were no conveniences that we have today. No inside plumbing, no bathroom, no running water, no washing machine, or electricity. She had to go to a spring to wash her laundry for her family. This was an all-day job. She cooked three meals a day on an iron cook stove, heated with stove wood.

She scrubbed wood floors and made quilts for the beds. We had no bedspreads, baby beds, baby strollers or baby carriers. If we went visiting in the neighborhood, we walked.

Mom was a thrifty person. When we were children and had fruit, she'd always save some. At her appointed time, she'd bring out a big apple or orange, peel it and divide it. It not only was a surprise but tasted better then, than what we previously had.

As long as Mom lived and was able to do her cooking, she always saved things many times that might have been thrown away.

Mom taught us children that anything that happened, it could have been worse. I didn't realize what all that meant then, as I do now. She was teaching us adaptability, appreciation, and to be realistic. She was also wanting us to have peace of mind, be positive, have happiness, have victory over all trials, contentment, a good attitude, and keep faith in our Lord Jesus.

My mom had no maids, no help with her children, except myself. However, the lovely, secure, exciting world of my childhood holds a distinct memory for me.

Last, but not least, we children were taught by Mom doing things, showing us how to do, and more than that, listening to us. We just knew she cared for each of us individually. None of us six children, that she raised to be grown, had the hang-ups that children have today. We all felt loved.

READING TO US

Mom would get all of us children on her bed and read to us. She read the Houston Chronicle news, then she'd read the 'funnies' for us. Sometimes she would read or teach us poems. Also, she read the Bible to us and told us about it. Perhaps this could have influenced me to love and appreciate books. Mom did not ever sit down and read a romance or any novel. She read through her Bible many times in her older age.

Sometimes she would sit down to read to us, and she would fall asleep. We would say to her, "Mama, you are going to sleep." I know she was so exhausted that when she could get still, she'd fall asleep.

DAD'S FINAL WEEKS

My dad's health was very bad and had been for several years. He had heart problems, plus several other major illnesses. He had had the first major vein surgery on both sides of his neck about 1970. He had to go to Houston for this surgery. The doctor there told him he could expect at least ten more years of life and he mentioned that factor several times. He was happy that he lived the ten years.

Then Dad had to have an appendectomy. As a matter of fact, his appendix had ruptured while he was in Mississippi at my house and by the time he got home, he was very ill. Dr. Walker performed this surgery. It was at this time that the doctor found that Dad also had a bad aneurysm. Dr. Walker performed this surgery about six or eight months later, along with stripping the veins in his legs and putting in new ones.

Anyway, Dad managed to get up and keep going until about seven weeks before he died. He was very ill, kept the pneumonia all those weeks. We all took turns staying with him day and night. Then one morning, on September 27, 1980, his life left him. This was a hard thing for all of us.

DAD'S FUNERAL

We buried Dad the next day because of circumstances concerning members of the family.

Dad was a person who loved people. During Dad's early years raising his family, we all worked all week long. Then about Saturday at noon, he would say "Let's go, kids. We are going visiting." He had an enormous amount of family and friends.

There seemed to be a houseful of people at Dad and Mom's every weekend. It wasn't unusual for Mom to set her table at least twice, many times more. This was a very long table.

It was to be much later that we realized that he was a much-loved man. There were many people at his funeral. Among the crowd we counted twenty-one ministers there to show their respect to the family.

Dad had some qualities that made people love him. He was not educated but he had a kind and loving heart. He really cared for people. He was a man of his word, dependable, no jealousy, generous, and he loved his family.

MOM'S LAST YEARS

Mom and I moved to Nacogdoches when Hershel passed away July 31, 1982. Mom's health was fair at that time. She already had Parkinson at that time. She was able to live in her apartment by herself. She lived in #141 and I (Hazel) lived catacorner from her in #146. She went to church regularly for five or six years.

Then she began to fall many times due to the Parkinson's. She had to have brain surgery due to a fall. She had several bad falls. We decided to just start staying with her round the clock. We made a schedule and all of us girls (Laverne, LaFaye, Elsie, Selvia, and me) stayed at our appointed time. We did this for four years at her apartment, then she had gotten to where it was almost impossible for us to handle her.

We had to make the hardest decision I ever made in my life to put her in a nursing home. This we did but we did still see her almost every day. When she was sick, we were there. She remained there for two years and seven months. She had been to the hospital so many times near the end that we chose to not take her back to the hospital. Mom had been on the feeding tube for seven months. She began to aspirate and just stop breathing. Faye and I were there in the room with her at her final breath. This death occurred September 8, 1994. She was 91 years old.

FAMILY OF ROBERT DANIEL LEE AND LILLIE LORENE HOOPER LEE

Name	Birth Date	Death Date	Age
Robert Daniel (Pa)	11-21-1903	9-27-1980	76
Lillie Lorene Hooper (Ma)	3-7-1903	9-8-1994	91
Hershel Robert(twin)	7-19-1925	7-31-1982	57
Hazel Iva (twin)	7-19-1925	5-27-2003	77
Elsie Vonciel	8-10-1927	11-1-2013	86
R. D. (triplet)	9-25-1928	3-23-1929	5 months
L.V. (triplet)	9-25-1928	7-27-1929	10 months
J.C. (triplet)	9-25-1928	8-2-1929	10 months
Laura Mae (twin)	5-25-1930	5-25-1930	less than 1 day
James Ray (twin)	5-25-1930	5-26-1930	1 day
Lillie LaVerne	10 26-1931	still living	
Baby Girl	1932	1932	miscarriage

Ella LaFaye	8-19-1934	still living	
Baby	1935	1935	birth (Ma had measles)
Jesse Washington	8-8-1940	9-4-2013	73
Kenneth Wayne	9-27-1945	9-30-1945	3 days

HAZEL IVA LEE PINKSTON

I am the daughter of Lillie Hooper Lee and Robert Daniel Lee. I was born at Jamesville, Texas, 3 miles east of Melrose, in Nacogdoches County. I weighed 4 lbs. I was born on July 19, 1925. I was a twin, and we were premature babies.

I did not finish high school, much to my regret. After the war started, Dad went to defense jobs and we older children got good jobs, too. It was more important to him at the time.

I was married to Cecil Raymond Pinkston on May 24, 1944.

MY BIRTH

I was born July 19, 1925, at 12:30 in the daytime. This was on a Sunday. It was a beautiful day for my mom, Lillie Lee, to have presented to her twins, a boy and a girl.

Hershel was born first with no problem, weighed in at 3 ½ lbs. I weighed 4 lbs. We were premature babies. It was a Dr. Brown who was the doctor that delivered us. He lived at Melrose, three miles away.

That evening all of the relatives on both sides came to see the new twins. Then all of the young people had a baseball game in the field nearby. This was something Mom never forgot. She was miserable and the whooping and yelling bothered her greatly.

Mom said I was a breech baby, which meant I came feet first. It was a difficult birth for Mom. The house that I was born in remained there for many years, thus I remember well seeing the house and place.

Remember back then there was no running water, no electricity, no baby food, no disposable diapers, no baby beds. Mom said she cooked turnip greens and used the pot liqueur from the greens to feed us with, because she did not give much milk by means of her breast.

God was with me, loved me even then, to let me survive.

HERSHEL ROBERT LEE

Hershel was my twin brother. He was born at Jamesville, Texas, 3 miles east of Melrose, in Nacogdoches County. He weighed 3 ½ lbs. at birth.

Hershel did not finish school, due to going to work. He held some good jobs during his life, but his health declined at an early age and his death came suddenly on July 31, 1982.

Hershel was married to Annie Belle Tyler in 1949.

MEMORIES OF HERSHEL

I have heard that twins are closer to each other than other siblings. This may be true. Hershel was very protective of me as a young lady. On the other hand, he had depended on me all his life. I suppose I was the cause of this, in part anyway. I always carried his books so he could romp and play with other kids on the way to school. I always thought that Mom petted him, but maybe because he was sickly many years, I'll never know.

I'd like to think that I had some good influence on him in his later years. I know he loved me, and I did him also.

I remember when our house burned, he came and was walking around in the house with me. I should say 'in the debris.' He said to me, "I don't know why this couldn't have happened to me instead of you." He was meaning that he didn't own a home, and I did have quite a nice home. It was paid for and all the furniture except I owed one payment on my refrigerator.

HERSHEL'S DEATH

Hershel had been in bad health for several years. He also had heart problems and sugar diabetes.

He was living with Mom at the time. This day I had gone to Nacogdoches to go to the sidewalk sale. Hershel was gone also. Perhaps he spent the night with Sarah, I'm not sure. When I got home, he was in bed. Mom told me that he had eaten and took his insulin to his room. I ordinarily would have gone down to the hall to talk to him, but I didn't.

I went to my trailor and put up my pretties that I had gotten for the children for Christmas. I was talking to LaNelle on the phone and Mom picked up the phone. She could hardly get her words out. She told me, "Come quick, Hazel. I think Hershel is dead."

This was such a shock for us. He had started to lie down but didn't even get his feet off the floor, was just partly on his bed.

ELSIE VONCIEL LEE WARD

Elsie was born at Aiken, Texas in Shelby County on August 10, 1927. Elsie, being one of the older children, did not finish school but went to work.

Elsie has done many good deeds to people everywhere she ever lived. The Bible speaks about using what you have for God. She has faithfully carried food to people all over the state of Texas where she's lived, saying nothing of inviting people to her homes. Elsie is such a good cook. I guess she got that from Mom. She has helped me so many times when I was in the hospital. She has been so very good to my children, in so many ways, when they were small and in later years also. Elsie has always been faithful to help me, as well as others.

Elsie married John Benjamin Ward on July 6, 1946.

LILLIE LAVERNE LEE WARD

LaVerne was born October 26, 1931, at Jamesville, Texas, 3 miles east of Melrose, in Nacogdoches County.

LaVerne is, in my opinion, the one of us girls who has more Godly wisdom. She has been a wonderful mother as well as grandmother to all her children. She surely will be remembered by them for all the unusual things she's done with them.

LaVerne went back and got her G.E.D. which none of us other girls bothered to do. "I'll never forget all the help you've done for me."

LaVerne married Aubry Willard Ward on May 22, 1950.

ELLA LAFAYE LEE JONES

LaFaye was born at Jamesville, Texas, 3 miles east of Melrose in Nacogdoches County on August 19, 1934.

Faye, as we call her now, is our baby sister. I think she inherited some of Mom's talents, concerning art and paintings. Faye has made some beautiful paintings. Faye has also worked in her church and for her

Lord faithfully all through her life. She now has a brand-new home that she literally helped build.

Faye has also helped me with my children when they were small and done many other good deeds for me, like taking me to see them married and for various reasons like coming so many times to Mississippi when Mark was injured and when I was in the hospital.

Faye married Leonard Dean Jones on July 26, 1950.

JESSE WASHINGTON LEE

Jesse was born about 3 miles south of Chireno, Texas in Nacogdoches County. He was born Aug 8, 1940. We were very proud to have a new brother. He was a delight.

Jesse had the privilege of going to school, but since Dad was a trader, farmer, and truck driver, Jesse learned what work was at a very early age, like us older children. Dad let Jesse drive, seemed like before he could see over the steering wheel. Jesse finished school and attended SFA (Stephen F. Austin State University) some. Jesse has had many different kinds of good jobs but being related to Robert Lee (ha-ha), he likes to buy and resell.

I thank the Lord that Jesse goes to church. "I thank you, Jesse, for all the personal things you've done for me through the years."

Jesse married Linda Joyce Martin on February 4, 1960.

BIG RED MEASLES

In the year of 1935, several people over the community had come down with the big red measles, which were very bad. Uncle George came to visit us, he was not aware that he was taking the measles, and Mom was expecting a baby. She had not had the measles herself.

All of us children took them, also Mom. We were very, very ill. We had high fevers, could hardly see, spent many days in bed.

About the time we were a little better, Mom went into labor to have the baby. It was not time for it, but Mom being so sick with the measles, she had a very difficult birth. We kids had to stay home because of the measles. They put us in a big back bedroom and closed the doors. I'm sure the others slept, but believe me, I prayed and cried all night. I was about 10 years old. After Aunt Pearl got the baby washed and dressed, she came to the door and called me. She told me the little baby only lived a few minutes and died. This baby was covered with those measles. I was somewhat relieved that my mom did not die.

Aunt Pearl made a coffin out of a shoe box, lined it pretty, put the little girl in it. Dad made a pine box. The weather was really bad, so Dad took the baby and buried it near the old house that was Grandpa Lee's old place. The 'Uncle Noah' house, we called it.

I remember Dad asking Mom if that would be alright to bury the baby there. She said, "I don't like for it to be put there." Meaning because it was not a cemetery. I guess under the circumstances Dad thought that was the best he could do. She never mentioned it again, as far as I knew.

MY BROTHER-IN-LAWS

DEAN JONES

Dean has been my brother for a long time. In fact, since 1950. I remember when Mom and Dad drove up in my yard, as they were returning from West Texas. I began to ask, "Where is Faye?" They told me, "She has gotten married." I immediately thought, "I like that!" Then I told Dad, "You would never have let me gotten married at 16 years of age." She was almost 17. The truth of the matter, I knew I was going to miss her badly.

Dean has been and still is a very good brother to me. He has always been a happy, contented, and outgoing person. Dean has worked hard on his career and dedicated to his work for the Lord.

"I won't forget how many times you and Faye have kept my children for me, for taking me places in more recent years, and mowing our yards at the farm. All of your good deeds will be recorded in Heaven. Thanks for helping me move and doing personal things for me."

AUBRY WARD

Aubry has been my brother since 1950 also. I personally think Aubry has been a good companion for LaVerne and a good Dad and Grandad to his grandchildren. Aubry has been a very hard worker. I know he's worked when lots of people would not have gotten out of bed.

"I also thank Aubry and LaVerne for the many times you all have kept my children for me. For all the ways you have helped me in time of sickness. I appreciate you, Aubry, for going to church with your family. It's paying off now as you see the harvest in your children and grandchildren. I will always remember you, for each time you left Mom and Dad's, you'd always say, "Let us know if you need us.""

J.B. WARD

J.B. has been my brother since 1946. "I think you, J.B., have been and still are, a very good Dad to all your boys. You got no education, but you worked very hard, in order for all your boys to have an education. I've heard Elsie say that you never had a run-in with any of your boys. That's certainly commendable on your part.

I know that Jesus keeps our records and that's the important thing in life, but I know also that many, many people in Nacogdoches watch you as you get out every week to sell for your church. Regardless of the hot or cold or rain, you are faithful to this work of the Lord.

I thank you and Elsie for all the times you've helped me with my children when they were small and otherwise. Thank you, J.B., for making my life easier by helping me in so many ways, namely, to move, run errands, fix my car, etc. For all the good meals you all have invited me to help eat. J.B, I'll never forget how you stayed in that hospital room with Dad, when things were so bad due to his being near death."

MY SISTER-IN-LAWS

ANNIE 'BELLE' LEE

I want to say that Belle has been my sister since 1949. Belle was a very hard worker. I'll never forget all the nice vegetables and fruit that she canned for her family. The things she put up in her freezer for winter.

Belle was an excellent seamstress. My, all those pretty dresses she made for her girls. Belle had 4 boys and 2 girls which I love very much. I don't get to see them as much as I'd like, but above everything, most important is them going to church and living for God, regardless if I see them down here. Perhaps we will meet in Heaven.

LINDA JOYCE LEE

Linda has been my sister since 1960. I'll never forget one cold day when Jesse and Linda came to my house. They had not been married very long. Then another time they came by, going to West Texas with their car loaded down with all their clothing or whatever. I gave them some canned vegetables. The main thing I remember was that Linda was taking her cat.

Linda has been an inspiration to me in many ways. She has also been a hard worker, bore 4 children, and been a good mother.

"I thank you for going to church and now raising your little grandchildren to know the truth and the importance of it. Thanks, and no forgetting how much you helped with Dad when he was so near death, and we could hardly stay by his bedside."

MY SPECIAL SISTER

SELVIA LEE ROBERTS BRADSHAW

Selvia was born September 8, 1923, meaning she is older than I am. Aunt Pearl Hooper (Mom's sister) was her mom. Selvia was born at Aiken, Texas.

Selvia came to Freeport and stayed with us, as we all worked together at the Camp Chemical Cafeteria. After I married, Selvia went back to Freeport and lived with Aunt Ella and Uncle Covy.

After Cecil died, I moved to Mississippi and lived there about 10 years. While I was living there, us girls all decided we'd have a little gathering of all our immediate family and do an adoption ceremony for Selvia to be our sister. She had been our cousin beforehand, but now she was our sister. I'd like to say that she has filled every expectation that we could have had or ever imagined.

When it became necessary for us girls to make a schedule for each of us to stay with Mom, Selvia was there every time until she had 3 strokes. She had those strokes at Mom's while staying the night and waiting on her.

Selvia had one daughter, Katherine Ann Bradshaw. She was born on November 14, 1948.

Kathy had one daughter also. Tisha Lynn Davis, born in February 1971. Tisha Lynn and her husband, Mike Jones, surprised the family by having twin daughters. Their names are Jori and Kelsey.

Postscript: Selvia passed on October 22, 2010 at 87 years of age, 7 years after the author.

LEE FAMILY

FAMILY OF JEPTHA WASHINGTON LEE

THOMAS SOLOMON LEE

Thomas Solomon Lee was born about 1750. He married a lady whose given name was Elizabeth. We don't know her surname. This man would have been my great great grandpa.

There was a tale that he killed a man who had been given an American Revolution Veterans land grant and was trying to claim his land. He was tried for murder and hung in Georgia, but they looked for records to verify this and could find none.

GREAT GRANDPA GEORGE (WASH) WASHINGTON LEE

This man would have been my great grandpa, 'Wash'. This was my Grandpa Jeptha Washington Lee's father. He was born on September 26, 1816 and died in December 1892 at the age of 76. He was buried in Lucas Cemetery, Salem community in Shelby County. He married Susanna Cole in 1845. She was born in 1830 in Mississippi and died in 1872.

GRANDPA JEPTHA (JEP) WASHINGTON LEE

This is my Grandpa 'Jep' Lee, my dad's father. He was born on September 2, 1871, in Jasper in Jasper County. He died October 23, 1950, at 79 years of age.

Grandpa Lee married Mary Francis Indiana Byrd in 1888. She was born on November 14, 1873, in Alabama. She died on May 4, 1935, at the age of 61 in Nacogdoches County. They are both buried at Cove Springs Cemetery in Nacogdoches County near Melrose.

GRANDPA LEE'S LIFE

Grandpa Jep Lee's mother, Susanna Cole, died when he was 15 months of age. He had several brothers and sisters who were older. Aunt Ella said she thought they just traveled around, kinda gypsy like. Can you imagine such heartache with a bunch of children and no mother? They finally settled in the Sardis community. This is not far from Aiken to the right of the hi-way.

One day Grandpa Jep passed by Grandpa Byrd's house and saw a girl sitting on the fence. He said, "I'm gonna marry that girl." He was 17 years of age. He asked for her and they were married soon. Grandma Indiana was 15 years old. They moved around awhile. Grandpa and Grandma went back to Jasper where he was born.

Their first baby was born around Conroe or Jasper. This baby was Archie Columbus Lee, born in December, 1889 and died in March, 1890. This baby was buried around Conroe.

Then they came back and settled around Salem. That's on up the road toward Center, off Hi-way 7 to the right. They settled on land, by the squatters right. Their cabin was made with poles and had no floor except dirt.

CHILDREN OF JEPTHA AND INDIANA LEE

UNCLE JESSE JAMES LEE

This was where the first child of Grandpa Jeptha and Grandma Indiana (Indie), Jesse James Lee, was born on February 13, 1891 in Nacogdoches County. Uncle Jesse married Johnnie Gertrude Blanton. She was born on January 16, 1891. Uncle Jesse died on June 15, 1951 at 66 years of age and was buried on Father's Day. Aunt Johnnie died February 25, 1985 at 94 years of age. They are both buried at the Swift Cemetery in Nacogdoches County. Cecil and I both thought lots of my Uncle Jesse and I think the feeling was mutual, as much as he visited us.

UNCLE HEBER BURTON LEE

The second child of Jeptha and Indie was Heber Burton Lee, born on January 26, 1894. Uncle Heber married Annie L. Knous, who was born October 24, 1897. I lived in Mississippi when Uncle Heber passed away on August 14, 1967 at 73 years of age. He was an outdoor person who loved to fish and hunt. Aunt Annie died on February 18, 1976 at 78 years of age. They are both buried at the Attoyac Baptist Church Cemetery in San Augustine County.

UNCLE NOAH SIMPSON LEE

Their third child, Noah Simpson Lee, was born on May 2, 1896. He was married to Minnie O. McKey, who was born on December 22, 1895. She preceded Uncle Noah in death on January 2, 1952 at 56 years of age. Then he went to live with Mom and Dad for many years. After we could keep him no more, he went to the nursing home. He lived there until his death on March 20, 1990 at 93 years of age. He and Aunt Minnie are both buried at the Lower Melrose Cemetery in Nacogdoches County.

AUNT ALMA LAUNA (LAEUNAH OR UNA) LEE MCKEY (MACKEY)

The fourth child was Alma LaUna Lee. She was born January 19, 1899. Alma married Daniel Jackson McKey in 1917. Uncle Dan was a cousin to Uncle Noah's wife, Minnie. Uncle Dan was born on February 14, 1897. Aunt Una died on May 4, 1925. I believe she had T.B. (tuberculosis). She left behind 5 young children, with the youngest being 9 and a half weeks old. This son died at 8 months of age. Uncle Dan then married Lillie Mae Fisher. Uncle Dan died on May 25, 1947 and Lillie Mae died on November 30, 1947 leaving 8 underage children from their marriage and 4 older children from his first marriage. They are all buried at Lower Melrose Cemetery in Nacogdoches County.

UNCLE FELIX LEE

The fifth child to be born was Felix, born on July 10, 1901. Felix died on September 16, 1904 at the tender age of 3. He is buried at the Lower Melrose Cemetery in Nacogdoches County. The cause of his death is unknown.

ROBERT DANIEL LEE (PA)

My dad was the sixth child born to Jeptha and Indie. He was born on November 21, 1903. He passed away on September 27, 1980 at 76 years of age. He was married to Lillie Lorene Hooper on November 22, 1924. She was born on March 7, 1903. She died on September 8, 1994 at 91 years of age. They are both buried at Cove Springs Cemetery in Nacogdoches County.

AUNT ETHEL MAE LEE KNOUS

The seventh child in the family was Ethel Mae Lee. She was born December 10, 1905. Her gravestone says November 10, 1905. She passed away on November 1, 1946 at 39 years of age. She married Henry Russell (Dick) Knous on August 9, 1924. He passed away on June 21, 1972 at the age of 70. Both are buried at the Lower Chireno Cemetery in Nacogdoches County. I remember Aunt Ethel having bad headaches many times. Also, her being so particular with the cleanliness of her children's bottoms. That's what I said! She'd check them each time. I guess Mom had too many to be so particular.

AUNT MEACY LEE GIPSON

Meacy Lee was the eighth child and the third girl born. She came into the world on February 2, 1908. She was married to William Clarence "Pat" Gipson, known as Uncle Pat to us. His birth date was July 31, 1904. Aunt Meacy died on April 27, 1952 at 44 years of age. They were living in West Texas. She had been ill for some time and got on her death bed. She wanted to come home to die. Uncle Covy and Dad went after her. She died in Memorial Hospital here in Nacogdoches. Uncle Pat has been dead for several years. He died on February 21, 1987 at 82 years of age.

I remember when Mom and Dad lived at the Nena Posey house on 95 South, not too far from Chireno. Uncle Pat and Aunt Meacy (Dad's sister) and Vonnie Mae (their daughter) came to their house. Aunt Meacy was sick then, in fact, she was in bed. Dad was all too happy for them to be there. Mom cooked and carried her meals to her bed and waited on her.

AUNT MEACY AFTER SURGERY

Aunt Meacy and Uncle Pat, along with Vonnie, moved to West Texas. They lived there when Vonnie met Buddy Jones and they were married. Buddy and Dean are brothers.

It seemed that Aunt Meacy was sick or ailing much of the time. She was finally diagnosed as having breast cancer. Her doctor out there suggested taking off her breast which she did have performed. She seemed to get some better but just about one year later, it re-occurred. She was very ill in a Lubbock hospital.

Uncle Covy, perhaps Aunt Ella also, went along, carried Dad out there, he didn't have a car. Aunt Meacy was glad they came, but she wanted to come home to die, so Dad said, "We will take you."

He went to the office and told them the situation of his sister wanting to come back home to die. They told him, "You can't take her." His reply was, "Why not?" They told him, "She owes a $500.00 hospital bill that will have to be paid." Dad said, "I'm going to pay it right now." which he did. Uncle Covy drove straight thru in record time to get her to the Lufkin hospital. Since she was so deathly ill, she stayed at the Lufkin hospital a few days. Some of the family wanted to bring her to Nacogdoches Memorial, the only hospital we had then. She lived a few more days and passed away. This was 1952.

My children were small, but I managed to help sit up with her some myself. I was there at the hospital the time she had the first seizure from pain. Aunt Meacy was alert and conscious just about to the

28

end. I never knew anyone could have known so many songs by heart, but she sung and sung. She talked about her funeral, as to what everyone would be wearing. It was a nightmare for all who sat with her.

Dad would not stay in her room, but Aunt Meacy knew he was there at the hospital, sleeping and eating in his truck. Dad was such a caring person and always helping someone.

AUNT VASTER MISSOURI "DOLLIE" LEE HOOPER

Aunt Dollie was born on January 5, 1911. She married George Napoleon Hooper, my mother's brother, who was born on September 13, 1908. Their wedding date was December 15, 1928. I remember that Aunt Dollie was one of the first ones to receive the Holy Ghost when Bro. Mott came to Jamesville. We would be out at the cow lot, and she would be talking about the Lord and start shouting and speaking in tongues, almost frighten me to death. Uncle George, I appreciate all the visits to see Mom and all the goodies you brought her. Aunt Dollie died on February 21, 1999 at 88 years of age and Uncle George died on June 26, 2005 at 96 years of age. They are buried at White Rock Cemetery in Shelby County.

AUNT ELLA SUE LEE LANGFORD

The youngest child and the fifth daughter, Ella Sue Lee, was born on December 4, 1917. She married Covy Charles Langford, who was born on June 10, 1917. They were married at our house, where Faye was born, in 1936. They had planned to be married somewhere else, but the weather was so bad, we had decided that Uncle Covy wasn't going to make it. I believe he had gotten stuck and had to walk the remainder of the way. He stopped at our neighbor and took a bath and dressed. Sister Brooksie Fitzgerald married them. Mom had prepared them a nice wedding supper.

Aunt Ella, I remember you washing and rolling my hair several times. I probably warted you because I liked to look pretty. Uncle Covy, I appreciate the things (money) that you gave me. May the Lord bless you even now, for the goodness you've shown to different people. Uncle Covy died on November 19, 1996 at 79 years of age. Aunt Ella died August 3, 2002 at 84 years of age. They are both buried at Cove Springs Cemetery in Nacogdoches County.

MEMORIES OF GRANDPA JEP LEE

He was a hardworking little man, not very tall but very industrious. He farmed, always had a good decent house to live in, had lots of horses, mules, cows, pigs, and chickens. They had a big fruit orchard. They raised lots of corn and other things in order to feed his animals. I remember in one of Grandpa's barns, he had a corn sheller. We would go up there and shell our corn to take to a grist mill, perhaps at Melrose.

Grandpa had a blacksmith shop. He fixed plows, hooved horses, and all those things that you do in a blacksmith shop. I can remember sometimes turning that blower for him to make the fire catch up.

I asked Aunt Ella how Grandpa acquired all the land he had at Jamesville. She told "In the beginning, he rented land from Mr. Whit Bently. Later, land was cheap. He brought land from or through the savings and loan." Grandpa was a good trader and manager, so I suspect he made many good deals through trading, whether it was horses and wagons for land or doing work for people for cash, like the blacksmithing was big business. I don't know how profitable it might have been.

Grandpa attended the Baptist church regularly and they all loved singing and playing of the organ at their home. Each one of Dad's brothers and sisters could sing and play. After the Holy Ghost was preached there, quite a few people received it. Mom said Grandpa Lee sought the Holy Ghost but never did receive it.

My Grandma Indiana Lee died at age 62 years. Grandpa Lee married Miss Myrtie later. She had gone to school with Dad and been a teacher to all of us. Now she was our step-grandmother. We all loved her, but it was different going to see Grandpa. I remember several years later Miss Myrtie went to Colorado to teach school, so Grandpa got up with Cecil and I and asked us to come and move him. We went and, after getting everything loaded and we got in the cab of the truck. Grandpa Lee said, in a broken voice, "Cecil, I've seen my happiest days here and I won't be happy anymore." This touched Cecil and me.

I can't recollect how long Grandpa lived after that, but I think he stayed with Dad and Mom part time. However, he bought the big two-story house in Chireno. Miss Myrtie came back before he died, but I don't know how close to his death. I am sure he had cancer.

Cecil sat with Grandpa one night at the hospital. They had tubes down his nose to drain the fluid off his stomach. Grandpa would pull them out. Someone had to stand by his bed and keep his hands down. This night, Cecil was obeying orders and Grandpa looked up at him and said, "Cecil, I would not do a dog like that." Cecil probably let him pull them out after that, knowing him. He loved Grandpa Lee.

GREAT UNCLE NATHANIEL LEE

This man was my Great Grandpa Washington Lee's brother. Great Uncle Nathaniel was born in 1809 in Georgia. He died in 1890 at age 80 or 81 and is buried at Chappell Cemetery, Petal, Forrest County, Mississippi. He was married to Sarah Chain Lee. They were married on January 19, 1830. She was born in 1815 in St. Tammany Louisiana. She died in 1860 at age 44 or 45 and is buried in the same cemetery.

GREEN BERRY LEE

Green Berry Lee was Great Uncle Nathaniel Lee's son and a cousin to Grandpa Lee. He was born on November 17, 1831 and died March 20, 1908. He died at age 76. He married Julia Ann Tyson about 1856. She was born on July 13, 1841 and died December 21, 1919. She was 78 years of age at death. They are both buried at the Old Leeville Cemetery in Forrest County, Mississippi.

Green Berry Lee was one of those men who didn't take 'no' for an answer. He didn't take a lot of time to make up his mind either, at least about important things, no-sir-ree! There's a community not far from Hattiesburg, Mississippi called Leeville. I'm not sure if it's called that now but perhaps. There's a whole flock of Lee's in Forrest County today, whom can be attributed to a snap decision he made while walking through an Alabama field one day before the Civil War.

According to family lore, Green Berry was returning from visiting relatives in Georgia when he passed a farm in Alabama and saw a lovely young lady working in the field. Green Berry decided that time and day that this young lady would be his bride. He went to the field she was working in and talked to her about marriage. She voiced no objections, so they went to another field to ask her father for permission to marry. Julie Ann Tyson's father must have been in for quite a surprise. He replied to Green Berry, "You don't want her. She has to be whipped often." He assured her father he could whip her if need be. He then brought the young lady back to Mississippi and married her.

Her grandson said as far as he knew she never saw her family again. This man said he had memories of her. Thus, Green Berry Lee and wife Julie Ann Lee were the original settlers of what is Leeville, Mississippi. This man said he could remember when almost every house in Leeville was inhabited by a Lee or a descendant. Floyd remembered when you could come all the way from Leeville to what is now the River Avenue Bridge leading into Hattiesburg and only pass four houses in all that area, known now as Petal. Hattiesburg was only a sawmill town.

GREAT UNCLE JESSIE J. LEE

Jessie was Grandpa Jephtha Lee's brother and my dad's uncle. He was born on December 9, 1859. He died on May 9, 1954 at 94 years of age. He was married to Nancy Ann Elizabeth Dufner who was born on June 3, 1870. She died on May 25, 1954 at 83 years of age. They are both buried in Koerth Cemetery in Koerth, Lavaca County, Texas. This man remembered when they came from Mississippi to Jasper, Texas in a covered wagon. He was older than Grandpa Lee.

FAMILY OF INDIANA BYRD LEE

GREAT GREAT GRANDPA GREEN BYRD

James Mitchel Byrd's father was Green Byrd, born July 4, 1805 and passed on February 7, 1894 at 88 years of age. He is buried at Old Salem Cemetery in Shelby County. His wife, the mother of James Mitchel Byrd, is unknown.

GREAT GRANDMA JAMIE MISSOURI BATTON BYRD & GREAT GRANDPA JAMES MITCHEL BYRD

My Grandmother was a Byrd, and her mother was Jamie Missouri Batton. Great Grandmother Jamie Missouri Batton was born in 1856 and died in 1923 at the age of 67. She was married to James Mitchel Byrd, born June 1, 1852 in Alabama. He died on April 22, 1922 at 69 years of age. They are buried at the Lower Melrose Cemetery in Nacogdoches County. Great Grandmother Jamie Missouri Batton's parents are unknown. Grandpa and Grandma Byrd had seven children.

GRANDMA MARY FRANCIS INDIANA BYRD LEE

Indiana was the first child born to James and Jamie Missouri Byrd. She was born on November 14, 1873. She died on May 4, 1935 at 62 years of age. She was married to Jeptha (Jep) Washington Lee. He was born on September 2, 1871 and died on October 23, 1950 at 79 years of age. They are both buried at Cove Springs Cemetery in Nacogdoches County.

GREAT AUNT ALLIE BYRD HOLMES

This lady was Grandma Lee's sister. Aunt Allie was born in September, 1891. She married Sam Holmes, who was Leonard Holmes's brother, I believe. He was born in February, 1886. Aunt Allie died in 1927 at the age of 35 or 36. She left five small boys. I assume he didn't think he could raise the boys, at any rate, Leanord was only a boy of about 16 years of age. He took the boys and raised them. He later married Corine Ackridge. She is still living. (She died in 2010.) Leonard Holmes died in 1974. Corine is my second cousin. Aunt Ella said this was sad to her. (Editor's note: In actuality, Leonard was the son of Aunt Allie and Uncle Sam. He was 16 or 17 when she died. There were 4 boys younger than him.) Allie and Sam, along with their son Leonard and his wife Corine, are all buried at Sardis Cemetery in San Augustine County.

HOOPER FAMILY

FAMILY OF CHARLES CARTER HOOPER

GREAT GRANDPA CLARK CHRISTOPHER NAPOLIAN "POLE" BONAPARTE MARSHALL MARION HOOPER

Grandpa Hooper's father was Clark Christopher Napolian "Pole" Bonaparte Marshall Marion Hooper. I don't wonder that they gave him a shorter name. I wish I could have known this man because he must have been an important man because of his long name.

He was born July 28, 1833 and died February 3, 1918 at 84 years of age. His first wife was Texanna Smith Hooper. She was born June 6, 1850 and died in 1889 at 38-39 years of age. She is buried at the Old Salem Cemetery in Shelby County, Texas.

After Texanna's death, Napolian married Latisha Mancil Hooper. She was born March 16, 1869 and passed away on May 4, 1938 at 69 years of age. They are buried at the Sardis Cemetery in San Augustine County, Texas.

Back when Grandpa Pole and his family lived, I don't guess it was too uncommon for people to not sleep on bedsprings. At least he didn't. Because of his rheumatism, he was unable to walk. My Grandpa Hooper, his son, would go and get his dad and bring him to their house for a visit every so often. Grandma and Grandpa lived down the lane at the old place. I remember the place well. I spent lots of nights there when Uncle Carter and his family lived there.

On one occasion, Grandma told Grandpa Pole, "I have a good bed fixed for you to sleep on." She told him she had put some bed springs on his bed. So, with her persuasion, he slept on them. She was sure he would rest better. The first night was fine. He agreed he had rested better. The second night he slept well, but upon waking, he sat on the side of the bed, as he was accustomed to doing, and began to rock himself in order to get himself up. This was not the correct way to have gotten up. The springs sent him sprawling in the middle of the bedroom. So, he told my grandma, "Never again will I sleep on bed springs." I guess the poor man only slept on a pair of bedsprings two nights of his life.

Also, my Grandma Hooper improvised a straight chair by putting wheels on each leg so Grandpa Pole could roll himself around over the house. He could not walk. This way he was not confined to any one place. Therefore, there has been a wheelchair in our family since back in the early 1900's.

GREAT UNCLE ED HOOPER

We knew this man as Uncle Ed. He was born Edward Steven Hooper on August 9, 1881 and died June 28, 1945. He is buried at White Rock in Shelby County, Texas. This was my Grandpa Hooper's brother. He was born blind. He lived with Grandpa and Grandma Hooper.

I remember him always sitting in a straight chair in the fireplace room. Although he was blind, he was a happy person. When it was wash day at Grandma's he always wanted to draw the wash water. The well had a big porch shed over it and they had steps going onto a platform and this was built right up beside and around the well. I believe my dad fixed this for them, so they didn't have to ever be in the rain while drawing water. Uncle Ed also carried in firewood. He could get around good from room to room by himself and to the table for meals. Sometimes Uncle Ed had seizures. I've seen him fall many times with one.

He learned scriptures by hearing them read to him. Uncle Ed could quote lots of scripture. He loved to go to church. He walked to White Rock to church with Selvia most every Saturday morning. They had services on Saturday morning at 11:00 A.M. Then he would go home with the Savel boys and spend the evening. Then they went back to church Saturday night and Sunday morning. Selvia went back on Sunday night. Sometimes someone would take them home but mostly they walked. Almost everyone walked. I'm not sure but it was at least two miles each way.

I remember Uncle Ed slept on a little iron cot. It had good mattresses on it. Grandpa helped him with his baths. Selvia helped him get dressed many times. People brought their babies who had thrush there for Uncle Ed to blow into their mouths. This seemed to work, don't ask me why or how.

Uncle Ed had a gift of prophecy to some extent. Selvia remembered different things. I am relating one incident. Selvia had wanted to go to a singing with some neighbors who lived nearby but someone came by and told her they were not going. Up in the afternoon, Uncle Ed told Selvia to get ready to go, these people would be by after her. She listened to him and got ready to go. Sure enough, they did come by for her.

GREAT UNCLE MONROE HOOPER

Uncle Monroe's father was N.B. Hooper or Great Grandpa Pole. This man was my Grandpa Hooper's brother. We do not know when he was born, or when he died, or where he was buried.

This is a true story that took place in Shelby County many long years ago, perhaps near 90 years or more (127 from time of publishing). Uncle Monroe was a young man at the time of this incident. Uncle Monroe and his dad had a saloon. At this time, there were not many white people around. The territory was all wilderness and full of wild animals, but more important was the fear of Indians that were very prevalent.

It was a cold, cold day in winter and an old man and a little boy came by Uncle Monroe's saloon. They were cold, wet, and hungry. Uncle

Monroe gave them food to eat, whiskey to drink, and let them warm by his fire until they were dry and rested. They thanked him and left.

Years later, the Indians were very hostile toward the white people because they were homesteading land which the Indians thought rightfully belonged to them. So, they went on the war path. Their aim was to get Uncle Monroe and another white man in the same general area of the community.

They captured Uncle Monroe and some of the Indians wanted to go ahead and scalp him right then and there. One of the Indians spoke up and said, "Let me stay here with this man and guard him." He instructed the others to go on and capture the other white man and bring him back and then they would kill them both at once.

He also told them, "I'll fire my gun three times if he tries to get away." So, it was a deal. After the band of Indians left, the Indian asked Uncle Monroe this question. "Do you remember years ago, when an old Indian man and a little boy came by your place and you gave them food, and whiskey and let them warm by your fire." "Yes," he replied, "I do." The Indian told him, "I am that little boy, and I won't ever forget the kind, good deed that you did for us. I am going to let you go free. I know these woods good. I am going to do something to make the others think that I shot you." He raised his breeches leg up and cut a long gash into his own leg and walked down one trail letting his blood drip along. He told Uncle Monroe, "You go due West. You see, I've dripped my blood due East. Now run, run as fast as you can. I'm going to fire my gun three times. They will come. I will tell them I shot you as you left westward."

By the time the Indians arrived, Uncle Monroe was a free man because he went west and lived to tell this story, but I don't know about the other man.

GRANDPA CHARLES CARTER HOOPER

Charles Carter Hooper was born on June 7, 1868. He passed on May 16, 1953 at 84 years of age. He was married to Mirtie Dell Hinkle Hooper who was born on June 23, 1876 in Peoria, Illinois. She passed on May 21, 1962 at 85 years of age. They are buried at White Rock Cemetery in Shelby County.

GRANDMA MERTIE DELL HINKLE HOOPER

Mertie Dell Hinkle was born June 23, 1876. She died May 21, 1962. She is buried at White Rock in Shelby County. This was my mom, Lillie Lee's mother. She was married to Charles Carter Hooper on June 23, 1894. Everyone called him. C.C. Hooper.

This was my dear, dear, Grandma Hooper. I remember her by many things. She wore her dresses to the floor, her sleeves to her wrist, and always had long hair.

She canned vegetables, jellies, and meat by the bushels. She enjoyed her pecan trees. She always had a little, small sack of pecans for all us children every Christmas. Sometimes, we'd think sure she'd forgotten to give them to us. You see, she was wise. She only gave these to us as we were leaving.

Grandma didn't whip you, but I've seen her sat down and talk to some of us grandkids and you'd rather had a whipping. Grandma used scripture when talking to us. One being "Reap what you sow." Another "Honor thy father and mother."

Grandma was born in Peoria, Illinois. She came to Texas in a covered wagon when she was 4 years of age. They first went to Waxahachie, Texas. They came to Texas due to her mom's health and to a warmer climate.

GRANDMA MERTIE HOOPER'S WEDDING DAY

One spring day in June, a long, long time ago, there was a young lady who had just turned 18 years of age, full of life and expectancy. She was in love with a nice-looking young man named Charles Carter Hooper. She was planning a get-a-way. You could call it running away from home.

She and Grandpa had talked of marriage, and he had already asked her father for her. He had agreed that Grandma could marry this young man. They had set the date for the 26th of June. Great-Grandma Hinkle evidently was not so eager for her daughter to marry so she was talking to Grandpa Hinkle about the situation. My Grandma heard her mom and dad talking to each other. They decided the best thing to do was to move completely out of the vicinity. The parents were not aware that she had overheard their plans.

Grandma had to act and act fast. She informed Grandpa and they made plans to elope. She had a new print dress, but she had torn a small hole in it. She decided she could mend the hold, this she did. She took her dress to the spring and left it. Grandma went about her chores as usual that morning. She went to the garden and gathered turnip greens. She took them to the spring and washed them but didn't take them back.

Guess what happened next? Her husband to be was there waiting for her as planned. They left without her parent's blessings. Evidently, Grandpa had a buggy for transportation so they could go to Center, Texas to get married. They were married the 23rd of June, 1894, at Center, Texas.

They ate their wedding supper at Aunt Mollie and Uncle Ike Mancil's home. They lived in the Sardis community at this time. Aunt Mollie was Grandpa Hooper's half-sister. Their menu was black-eyed peas, turnip greens, and cornbread. Later the Mancil's moved to the settlement just off 103 which is called the Wilson settlement today.

My mom traveled in a wagon from Aiken, Texas to their home visiting as a child many times.

Great-Grandma and Great-Grandpa Hinkle were not too hard on them. They did not move and accepted the newly wedded couple.

GRANDPA HOOPER WALKING TO CENTER

My Grandpa Hooper would get up and leave at daybreak and start out to Center to buy groceries. This distance was 13 miles one way. Sometimes someone would come along and give him a ride, but many times he walked all the way and back. I think he only got the bare necessities when he walked this far.

He sometimes walked to another store which was only 4 miles one way and bought groceries and carried them home to Aiken. 10# flour, 10# sugar, and coffee. Mom said just a regular bill of groceries that he bought and carried on his back.

VISITING GRANDPA AND GRANDMA HOOPER

We visited our grandparents here at Aiken quite often. Dad was good to take Mom to see her parents. He loved them, too. We lived near his people in their early years of marriage, so he felt it his duty to visit there also.

Grandpa and Aunt Pearl (Selvia's mom) ran a store at Aiken. They had everything in it, barrels of vinegar, barrels of beans, rice, flour, and sugar. They had kerosene and a gas station. All kinds of candy and groceries were there.

Grandpa was a constable in Shelby County several years. He was a very witty person. I wish I could remember all the true stories I've heard them tell around his fireplace.

41

When we started to eat at Grandpa's table, it was strictly for that purpose. We were not allowed to talk at his table. My, how many things we could think of to say, but couldn't say them. Sometimes we'd get so tickled, we'd have to leave the table. No, I don't mean he was ugly or boisterous with us. It was a funny rule, but it was his way of respect. We could ask for food by saying, "May I" or "Thank you for so and so."

When we drove up in front of their house, if Grandpa was there you could depend on him to meet us at the gate and kiss every one of us with his long beard.

CHARLES AND MERTIE HOOPER'S CHILDREN

AUNT MERTIE FRANCIS HOOPER

Mertie Francis Hooper was Mom's oldest sister. She was born on July 31, 1896 at Aiken, I assume. I know she was born in Shelby County. She died on December 30, 1977 at 81 years of age. She is buried at White Rock Cemetery in Shelby County.

She was a pretty, young lady. She finished school, then something happened to her. She was so nervous that she occupied a room alone and Grandma took her meals to her room. Sometimes we got to see her when we visited, sometimes we did not.

Aunt Francis outlived Grandma, Grandpa, and Aunt Pearl. Her health improved somewhat in her later years. She died a mysterious death. She could hardly walk across the floor. She lived by herself. Then one cold, cold freezing morning, someone went to check on her. I believe it was Uncle Carter, her brother. I think he had dreamed about her that morning. Seems as if another member of the family had also been awakened during the night concerned about her. They found her body out in the field a ways from the house.

She was fully dressed, her clothing was pulled down, and she had her shoes off. They were sitting side by side at her head. I was the one who found her keys quite some distance from her body. She was supposed to have had some money, but not much was found. The coroner report was that she had probably suffered a stroke. We'll never know.

Postscript: Mom told me in later years of my life that she thought Aunt Francis' bad health was because of not being able to marry a boy she loved. For what reason, she didn't seem to be sure, if he jilted her or if Grandpa forbid her to marry him. I'll never know that, either.

MY VISIT TO AUNT FRANCIS ABOUT 1976

I came home to live again, after living in Mississippi for about ten years. I moved my mobile home, I should say Charles moved it at his expense, back down to the farm to be near Mom and Dad and help them.

One night I dreamed that I went to spend the night with Aunt Francis. I told Mom I was going and, if she acted as if she'd like for me to stay, I would. I had gone prepared to stay overnight. It was very hot summertime. I knocked on the door nearest her room. She finally came to the door. She was very glad I'd come to see her.

She told me, "Hazel, come on in here and I'll get you a fan." I thought she meant an electric fan. Guess what? She handed me one of those kinds that the funeral homes or some businesses used to give away. One you had to fan by hand to make any resemblance of wind.

Anyway, we visited all evening. It began to get late. She said, "Hazel, why don't you spend the night with me?" I said, "Aunt Francis, I believe I will." She then told me, "I'll let you sleep in my room because it's cooler in there."

43

Elsie said she would not have slept in there for any amount of money. I didn't mind to sleep in her room and I felt privileged to sleep on her bed. The traffic kept me awake quite a bit since I was used to little or no traffic at night at the river.

Aunt Francis told me before we went to bed that she didn't rest well at night and often times she had to get up and walk around." She didn't want me to think there was a burglar in the house. I did not hear her all night so the next morning I asked her, "Aunt Francis, did you rest well last night?" She replied, "I reckon I did. I slept like a log, not even waking up all night long."

She asked me to go to the store for her, down at Lillie Mae, below White Rock. She fixed our breakfast while I was gone. I went home feeling like I had obeyed the Lord, thus making her happy and me, too. Aunt Francis died December 30, 1977, the next year after I stayed the night with her.

AUNT PEARL "PEARLEY" ANN "PIRTY" HOOPER ROBERTS

Aunt Pearl was a real standby for Grandpa and Grandma Hooper. Aunt Pearl was all over the place. She was quick and running from their home to the store and back, no telling how many times a day.

Aunt Pearl kept busy cooking food, hanging clothes, feeding the chickens, milking the cow, gathering fruits and vegetables, helping to do anything that needed to be done. Aunt Pearl always had big pockets on her dresses, and she always had candy or gum in her dress pockets. I could not imagine how she always knew when we were coming.

At Christmas, when we went, she always tried to get "Christmas Eve gift" on us first.

So many times, when Mom was sick, or some of the family, Dad would go to Aiken to fetch Grandma or Aunt Pearl. Surely there will be a reward for people who have helped others so very much. Aunt Pearl had so many friends, people all over Shelby County knew her and Grandpa Hooper.

Aunt Pearl was what we called her, but her christening name was Pearley Ann Hooper. She was born November 20th, 1898, and died August 8th, 1970, attaining the age of 71 years. She is buried at White Rock Cemetery in Shelby County.

Aunt Pearl took rheumatism in her arms very badly, then she was hit by a car while walking on the side of the hi-way and drug up the road. I remember Aunt Pearl by all the beautiful quilts she made and quilted by hand. She had a huge quilt box full of pretty quilts at one time.

AUNT ALLIE ADALINE HOOPER WOOD

Aunt Allie was born on March 10, 1901 and died on April 26, 1991 at 90 years of age. She was married to John W. Wood, who was born on July 16, 1898 and died on October 20, 1978 at 80 years of age. They are buried at Hobart Rose Cemetery in Kiowa County, Oklahoma.

LILLIE LORENE HOOPER LEE (MA)

Lillie Lorene Hooper was born March 7, 1903. She was born at Aiken, Texas in Shelby County. She was the daughter of Mertie Dell Hinkle Hooper and Charles Carter Hooper, known as C.C. Hooper. She married Robert Daniel Lee, on November 22, 1924. She passed on September 8, 1994 at 91 years of age. She is buried, along with her husband, at Cove Springs Cemetery, Nacogdoches County.

UNCLE CARTER G. HOOPER

Uncle Carter was born on Jan 8, 1906 and passed on February 24, 1997. He was married to Verniece L. Hooper in 1928. Her birthdate was February 15, 1909 and she passed on May 11, 1991 at 82 years of age. They are buried at White Rock Cemetery in Shelby County.

UNCLE CARTER GETTING US A CHRISTMAS TREE

One Christmas, Uncle Carter asked us kids if we would like to go cut a sure enough big Christmas tree. Oh, were we thrilled! I know Selvia and all us children went, down in Grandpa's pasture, near a ravine or such. Uncle Carter sawed and sawed, finally felling the tree. This was a cedar tree. It took us a long time, with lots of pulls and pushing to get that tree to Grandma's house.

He put it in the corner of the fireplace room. It went all the way from floor to ceiling. I never saw a tree that big at Grandma's before or since. Then we all decorated it with whatever we had. I'm sure strung up popcorn. You see, a lot of the brothers and sisters lived nearby so all were invited to bring their gifts and children. We opened those gifts on Christmas morning.

No, I don't remember what any of the gifts were, but that tree is indelible in my mind. We always had much good food at Grandma and Grandpa's at Christmas times. So much fun and such happy memories for all of us.

UNCLE GEORGE NAPOLEON HOOPER

George Napoleon Hooper was born on September 13, 1908. He married my dad's sister, Aunt Dollie, who was born on January 5, 1911. Their wedding date was December 15, 1928. Aunt Dollie died on February 21, 1999 at 88 years of age and Uncle George died on

June 26, 2005 at 96 years of age. They are buried at White Rock Cemetery in Shelby County.

UNCLE WILLIAM 'WILLIE' EDWARD HOOPER

Uncle Willie was born on November 14, 1910. He married Pearline Parrish Hooper who was born on January 3, 1916. He died on May 18, 1976 at 65 years of age. His wife died on January 23, 1978 at 62 years of age. They are buried at White Rock Cemetery in Shelby County.

AUNT JEWELL HOOPER CHANDLER BROWN

Aunt Jewell was born on February 16, 1913. She married Ivy Ely Chandler on March 19, 1903. Ivy passed on April 21, 1958 at the age of 55. Jewell remarried to a man named Brown. After she passed on January 20, 2008 at the age of 94, she was buried next to Ivy at White Rock Cemetery in Shelby County.

HINKLE ANCESTORS

GREAT GREAT GRANDPA AND GRANDMA HINKLE

My great granddaddy was Daniel J. Hinkle. He was born in 1820 in Ohio. He died at an unknown date and age and was buried at Hinkle Cemetery in Peoria County, Illinois. His wife, Bandena "Tenn" Shreffler Hinkle, was Grandma Hooper's grandma. She was born on April 29, 1826, in Illinois. She died on January 10, 1909, at age 82 and is buried in Sardis Cemetery in San Augustine County.

GREAT GRANDPA DANIEL GEORGE HINKLE

Daniel George Hinkle was Grandma Hooper's father. He was born January 1853 and died December 25, 1918, at 65 years of age. He married Bennie Francis McGraw Hinkle. She was born in 1856 and died in 1919 at age 62-63 years. They are buried at Sardis Cemetery in San Augustine County.

His brothers were John, Charlie, and Levi Hinkle. His sister was Orline Hinkle.

Great Grandpa Hinkle was a stout healthy-looking man, but he evidently had heart problems. One morning he got up and went to the barn to milk the cow. He was gone longer than usual. Grandma Hinkle went to the barn to check on him. She found him fallen on the ground with his head in a little puddle of water. He was in the hallway of the barn. This was on a Christmas day.

Grandma rushed back to the phone. Mom and Aunt Pearl were running the switchboard at Aiken, Texas. Aunt Pearl received this call about their great grandpa. They rushed across the hi-way, going to the store to get help to get him into the house.

Mom said that she knew Mr. Euel Hopkins was one man who assisted. Also Mr. Dave Duke with was Sister Alders father.

Mom stood at the foot of his bed and heard him say, "I see Ma." Grandma Hooper asked him, "What did you say?" He repeated the statement, "I see Ma." In a short time, he was dead, supposedly from a heart attack.

GREAT GRANDMA BENNIE FRANCIS MCGRAW HINKLE

My Grandma Hooper's mother, which would be my great-grandmother, was born Bennie Francis McGraw. This lady, my Great-Grandma Hinkle, had a restaurant in Illinois. At some time

48

during their traveling, Mom said they stopped at San Augustine, Texas and she ran a rooming house there. Mom pointed the house out to me several times. Perhaps they had a restaurant there also. Then on to Shelby County. I think this is where my Grandmother Hooper met my Grandpa Hooper.

Bennie Francis Hinkle was the daughter of John C. McGraw (Col.) who is my Great-great-grandpa McGraw. Her mother was Mary Ann Hixon. Mary Ann Hixon was married to John C. McGraw for the first time, then he left her. Selvia said she thought he was a United States Marshal, and he wanted my great, great-grandmother to travel with him and she refused. Later, she married Mr. Joseph Eads. Her children by Mr. Eads were Jim and Belle Eads. They were Great Grandma Hinkle's half brother and sister.

Great-Grandma Bennie Francis McGraw Hinkle had 3 brothers; Will, Douglass, and John McGraw, and perhaps another brother.

One time, this lady wanted to go to a dance. Her parents would not let her go, so she made a way. She tore up a sheet, tied the strips together, and jumped out the window and went anyway. She had put on her Daddy's coat and put all his medals and pins of distinction on this coat. Some young man there was really impressed with that coat (perhaps it was her) and he asked if he could take her home from the dance. She was obliged.

GREAT UNCLE GEORGE WILLIAM HINKLE

My Grandma Hooper's brother was George William Hinkle. We all called him Uncle Will. I don't think he visited Grandma often, but he did come occasionally. Dad and Mom visited them, along with us children several times. They lived at Pineland, Texas. It seems only a skip now, but then it was a long way. Uncle Will and Aunt Callie's children were Horace Hinkle, Hollis Hinkle, Bennie Dell Hinkle Wright, Estelle Hinkle Little, and Ozelle Hinkle McHahon.

These children and my mom, Lillie Lee, were first cousins. We hear from some of these folks. They attend the Hooper reunions.

BONNIE PARKER AND CLYDE BARROW

My sister-in-law, Linda Martin Lee, has heard her mom, Mrs. Grace Martin, speak of the Parker sisters. Mrs. Martin lived nearby them; they played together. Bonnie even spent the night with Grace when they were young. Mr. John Dee Martin, Linda's father, was said to be related to Clyde Barrow. Linda Joyce's uncle, Ford Smith, remembered them well.

I don't guess I ever saw them, but they were at Dee Brown's joint before they died. My Daddy and Uncle Willie were at Dee Brown's joint. Dee Brown asked Dad if he would deliver a gallon of whiskey to the Bonnie and Clyde gang. Dad did deliver this and was paid in silver dollars. This was about 6 or 8 months before they died.

My Granddaddy Hooper and Aunt Pearl ran a store and service station combination. Bonnie and Clyde came by one day and stopped at the gas pumps. Aunt Pearl went out and gassed up the car. She looked straight into the back seat of the car and saw Bonnie with a big, long shotgun laying across her lap. They hurriedly gave her a big bill, told her to 'keep the change' and sped off. They were outlaws and it wasn't long before they were killed.

In 1972, my brother, Jesse Lee, and my son, Charles Pinkston worked in Arcadia, Louisiana for a Mr. Jordan, which was the brother of the sheriff, a Mr. Henderson Jordan of Bienville Parish, Louisiana, who was part of the group that killed Bonnie and Clyde.

It was said that Bonnie and Clyde were living with a family and were helping them by giving them money. The day they were killed, these same friends were the ones to betray them. They ratted on them; told the road they were to be travelling on that early morning of May 23, 1934. The friend parked his car in the road and pretended to have a flat. He tried to stop Clyde. When he came over the hill, someone else asked them to stop but they would not stop, so they started shooting and killed both Bonnie and Clyde.

MY PERSONAL MEMORIES OF CHILDHOOD

MY VERY FIRST MEMORY OF ANYTHING

I remember us living at a little house when I was two and three years old. I remember Hershel and I running and playing in a real picturesque place. It had a gulley on it. It was fun, also I remember us looking for hens' nests and then we'd take the eggs to Mom.

WORKING IN FIELD AT AGE 3 OR 4

When we were too small to use a hoe, Dad would give us a row of vegetables or cotton and have us pull the grass up. We loved to do it. This was teaching us responsibilities.

MOM'S HELPER

Little did I know that soon I was to be my mom's little helper. Mom was not well and, either through miscarriages or natural births, it seemed she was sick most of the time. She began to depend on me to help her. Responsibilities came to me because of an urgent necessity.

When Faye was only five or six months old, Mom had to wean her because she was pregnant again. Faye would not take a bottle to drink any kind of milk. Dad got all kinds of milk; she would not take it. We had a small rocking chair. I sat up at night, sometimes almost all night, and rocked her. Also, I was in school. It worried Mom really bad, but she couldn't take her, she wanted to nurse. Incidentally, Faye has never drank milk.

I can recall so vividly of Mom being sick. I was so little, but I'd go beside the chimney and pray for her. It was my helplessness that caused me so much pain. I was so sensitive to Mom's needs.

WORRY

How vividly I remember when I was about five years old. There was talk about war. My ears always caught everything, especially when I knew, from the looks on Mom and Dad's faces, that they were very concerned. This gave me reason to be worried, I thought.

I recall Mom being out in the garden getting vegetables to cook and my pulling on her dress tail, asking about this thing called war. I just knew if there was a war, my dad would have to go. Mom assured me there probably would not be a war and it wasn't for many years.

Another time the weather was bad. It had rained all day and was still raining when night came. We children had gone to bed, but Mom was sitting up rocking one of the children and I knew she was worrying about Dad. Dad was driving a grocery truck, which he owned. He went everywhere and there were no paved roads. During rainy weather, the roads became impassable.

I got up and asked about Dad. She told me "He'll probably be spending the night with someone because of the roads," and he did. I remember when Highway 21 was paved. I sometimes now wonder if my being a worry wart helped to ease Mom's pains or made them worse. I sure did pray for my mom and my dad so many times when I was very small.

PHONOGRAPH

I remember the day Dad came home with this big old box. We wanted to know what the thing was. He soon told us and showed us how to work it.

It was a big old hand cranked phonograph. We got lots of pleasure out of that music box. We soon learned the songs on all the records. This was before we had a radio. I don't remember any of the songs except "She'll Be Coming Round the Mountain When She Comes", an old hillbilly song.

UNPLEASANT MEMORY

One unpleasant memory, in the depression years, the government ordered a certain number of cows killed. They killed them in front of our house. I can still remember the bellow of those cows. The people were paid $25.00 each to kill the cows.

TRAGEDY

One time I did not mind my mom, I didn't think she would ever know about it, but she did. We had some relatives in Shelby County who had been murdered. This was the year of 1934 in October. These were two boys who were cousins. Their names were Lonnie Hooper (16) and Ewell Hooper (20). Lonnie was my Great-Aunt Ada Byrd Hooper's son; she was Grandma Lee's sister. His dad was my Great-Uncle Jesse Hooper; he was Grandpa Hooper's brother. (Lonnie was Pa's first cousin from the Lee side & Ma's first cousin from the Hooper side.) Unknown exactly how Ewell was related.

This was big news all over several counties. The Houston Chronicle was full of the news everyday about this double murder. They had been shot in a house, we were quite sure and then someone had carried their bodies way down in the woods and placed them beside some logs and covered them with brush.

Since this was direct family to us, Dad sometimes learned new factors concerning it before it hit the papers. On this occasion, he had come telling Mom and us what he had heard. Mom told me the next morning before going to school to be sure and not tell what I knew about the murders. I'm sure she thought I'd be apt to tell my teacher, Mrs. Effie Fowler. Sure enough, I did. I don't know if she questioned me or if I volunteered and told her the new news. That afternoon I had already gotten home from school and Mrs. Effie walked by our house from school to her house. Would you believe that Mom was out in the yard and Mrs. Effie stopped and told her, "Hazel told me about the new news you all heard about Lonnie and Ewell." I don't remember if I got a spanking or not, but I sure deserved it.

STORMS AND STORM CELLARS

Dad was in a tornado when he was a young man. He was at church at Melrose and the storm took the church away and just left the church floor there. He said it blew trees down around where everyone had their horses tied. I don't recollect if it killed any horses or not.

At any rate, Dad was so afraid of a bad cloud that he always dug a storm cellar wherever we lived. I guess he passed his fear to me because I was fearful, even if it was lightning 50 miles away. I was always happy to go to the storm cellar. I felt safer there.

One night we were in the storm cellar, along with Uncle George and Aunt Dollie and family. It was a very bad storm, especially electric storm. Every now and then Dad and Uncle George would peep out the storm door and look at the weather.

I'll never forget that they looked up toward Grandpa and Grandma Lee's and saw something burning. They left us in the cellar and went to investigate things. Lightning had struck Grandpa Lee's huge barn and it was filled with hay and corn. Aunt Ethel and Uncle Dick were there visiting that night and it burned up their pair of big fine horses, also other stock.

My Grandma Lee was near death at this time. They were preparing to take her to the schoolhouse because of the tremendous fire, but they didn't have to do that. Grandma had cancer. She also had the Holy Ghost.

God was so good to them to not let their house burn. I was by there this past week, February 1995, and the chimney to the house has fallen down but the house is still there. My Grandma died there and had her funeral there because of torrential rain at the time. It had actually washed the dump out at the bottom of Jamesville Hill. No traffic could go to Melrose. She was buried at Cove Springs. Many memories went with the burning of that barn. This was in 1934.

I LOVED TO WORK

At an early age, I began to appreciate time. I always wanted to be on time. I always felt like I had to be constantly hurrying the other kids to get ready and us get to the bus stop on time to catch the bus. I was very impatient with them.

We always had chores to do, inside and outside. Such things as feeding cows, horses, hogs, and chickens. We had to get water for cooking and bathing. Sometimes we had a well nearby and other times we had to carry water from a spring. There was stove wood and firewood to bring in. Sometimes it meant splitting the stove wood.

TEETH

When I was about eight or nine years of age, I took a bad, bad sore mouth. My teeth were loose and my gums very sore. Dad carried me to the dentist at Nacogdoches several times. He gave me medication. It got worse. We went back about the third time. My teeth were so loose, you could pick them up. The dentist put a towel around my neck to pull all my teeth. Then he told Dad, "I hate so bad to pull her teeth. I am going to try another medication." That helped considerable, but I always had problems with my teeth being loose. I always believed that was a factor in having to get dentures at age forty-three. We never knew what caused the problem.

DIPHTHERIA

In the year 1930 or 1931, we moved two miles off the main Jamesville Road, to a place we nicknamed "The Red Land Place" and that's exactly what it was, red, red land.

We had a neighbor family who lived on the hill from us. One of his little boys took very ill. My Dad would go up there and sit awhile with this family every night. They thought this child just had 'croup'.

One cold, cold night, Dad came home very late and began to put wood in the fireplace. Then he took all his clothing off and put it in the fire. Mom asked him, "What are you doing?" He then had awakened us children telling us that the child had died, and he was sure he had diphtheria. The child was four years of age. His name was Ira Ballow.

The next day, Dad took all us children to Nacogdoches to get us preventative shots. We went back home, but in a short time, Hershel and I became very ill. So, Dad told Mom, "We need to go to Papa and Mama." They lived in the big house near the school. The roads were more passable up there. We were very, very ill. I was so bad that I did not know much of anything for days. I had such high fever.

Dad went after the doctor to come to the house. He gave me the second shot and said, "This will either kill her or make her better." This shot cost $25.00.

I did get somewhat better. We were seven years of age and in school. I very well remember that on Christmas Day, they wanted us to get up and go to the table for Christmas dinner. We got up and could not walk. We literally had to learn how to walk again.

NO LAWN MOWERS

People kept their yards free of grass. Don't ask me how. We used brush brooms to sweep our yards. The yards were very hard packed and quite pretty. The only thing, it meant sand tracking into the houses. That didn't matter too much either because there were no carpets or linoleum. The brush brooms were made from willow bushes. It was on these hard, pretty yards that we drew our hop-scotch patterns. We jumped on one foot to the designated blocks. The one who got to the finishing block was the winner.

DOING MY FIRST WASHING IN WASH POT

By the time I was ten years old, I felt myself enormously advanced in age and experience. I no longer thought of myself as needing protection. I had begun to have my own protective feelings. I felt responsible to help my mom, my twin brother Hershel, and the other children. Mom actually depended on me.

About this time, 1934, we had a new baby sister. LaFaye was born. Dad could not get in touch with the black lady who usually helped Mom at times like this. I told Mom, "I'll wash the clothes." She didn't think I could, and more so, she didn't think I should, because of it being sheets and things used during the birthing of Faye. Mom gave me instructions of just how to do for this occasion. Dad built the fire around the washpot for me, and I did all the rest by myself.

Then we had company and Elsie and I cooked a big meal for a lot of people. I did not feel that we were being mistreated by doing this.

RETURNING MY PRETTY SCRAP

On a hot summer day, Mom, and all of us children went to visit our neighbor. It was about a half mile uphill all the way. The ground was very rocky and graveled. We children were barefooted which made walking bad.

When we reached the neighbor's house, she was gone so we had to turn around and go right back home. As we were in the yard, I saw a pretty piece of scrap printed material, probably the size of a 3- or 4-inch square, laying on the ground in front of her house.

We got almost down the hill and Mom spied the scrap in my hand. She said, "Hazel, where did you get that?" I told her. She said, "You'll have to take it back. That is called stealing." She instructed me to put it back in exactly the spot where I had gotten it. She told me, "We'll wait for you." My, how long that trip back was to me.

This was a great lesson in life for me. From that day to this, I have never taken anything that didn't belong to me without asking. I had many jobs when I was working in the public, most all of them involved money. I was very trustworthy.

It's odd that one can recollect so many memories from childhood. I think we remember happy occasions, and, very vividly I think, fear. Really, I do remember many unhappy, unpleasant times and with much pain, but it's hard for me to recapture these things. Perhaps I don't want to. I do think that Jesus wants it to be that way because He tells us in His word, "To think on the good things, if there be any." And there are many good things.

Postscript: Incidentally, looking back to that pretty piece of print material, I am sure of one thing. My tastes have remained about the same. What I liked then as a child, I still love today; pretty material, cooking, and working. (1995) I have been able to satisfy my desire for material to make things with. I have also cooked thousands of dollars' worth of fried pies for churches, here, there, and everywhere, which I loved to do

DAD GOES TO SOUTH TEXAS

Probably in the year 1934 or 1935, Dad carried his dad to see some of his people who lived in South Texas. This was my Granddaddy Lee that he took. They were gone several days, and when he returned home, he told us children that Grandpa Lee had brought something that was a strange looking creature from South Texas.

They lived up the road from us a short distance, so we said, "Let's go!" Dad said, "Wait a minute. He's going to charge you 10 cents each to see this creature." So, our countenances fell. Then he replied, "I'm going to give you the money to go see it."

Off we went to see what it was that Grandpa Lee had, that was such a curiosity. When we told him we had our money and had come to see whatever it was he had brought back to show us, he started laughing, telling us, "Yes, I do have something that's really strange looking but I'm not charging you children to see it." In other words, Dad was playing with us. He had brought home some 'horned toads' which up to that time no one had ever seen a horned toad in East Texas. We really did think it was a neat, strange creature.

FOURTH OF JULY PICNICS WHEN WE LIVED AT JAMESVILLE

When we children were small and growing up, the Lee family always went to the Tupple Gum Slough for a big Fourth of July get-together. Dad oftentimes carried a barrel with cold soda pops iced down, along with watermelons and food goodies. The main attraction for most of the family was fishing. I remember one time that Grandma Lee was walking along a foot log and slipped and fell. This hurt her leg very badly. She was crippled with it for some time. I think the nearest I ever came to dying from thirst was at one of these grand picnics. I think the water there wasn't good to drink and we had gotten out of water, but we survived.

MOVING DAYS

My, how I still think of moving days. Sometimes we moved, at least in part, on a wagon. Dad always had an old pickup and, if not, he would buy a big old car and cut the back off of it, thus making what we called a 'hoopie'. You see, he'd put a flat bed with little 3- or 6-inch boards on the sides and haul anything from children to furniture to farm needs.

Our furniture consisted of the bare essentials of life. This included iron bedsteads, bed springs, slats, mattresses, homemade table for eating on, other small tables, and benches. The big item was the quilt box. I always wondered why they called this the quilt box when, in reality, it was where we put all the sheets, underwear, towels, washcloths, etc. We also had the cookstove with all those old sooty pipes. Of course, our pots and pans, wash pots, and dishes, etc.

The biggest part of moving was the plow tools, cultivator, disc, harrows, etc. The chickens had to be caught the night before and put in a coop. Then the horses, cows, and pigs penned and moved.

These times my dad's patience did get pretty thin. He'd yell and holler at us to come and help unload. I'm sure we were always in our new house looking it over.

Then the next morning we'd wake up and be in a brand-new place – I mean a different place. Actually, we mostly lived at Jamesville, but I can remember six different farms that we lived and farmed. I am going to attempt to recall places I lived from birth to present.

1. The first place I lived at was at Jamesville, TX, three miles east of Melrose, TX. This was off the Jamesville Road to the left coming from Melrose. It was a little long shotgun house, as they were called. This house was there several years; thus, I remember it well. Hershel and I were born on July 19, 1925, at 12:30 daytime at this place.

2. Mom and Dad moved back to Aiken in Grandma and Grandpa's house on Highway 7 toward Center. I'm sure this move was made because Mom needed help since Hershel and I were so small. Elsie was born here on August 10, 1927. I don't remember living here.

3. We moved back to Jamesville on the Mount Gillion Road near Jamesville. Uncle Hebron and Aunt Annie lived across the road from our house at this time. Later on, Aunt Dollie and Uncle George lived at this place. Their daughter, Pauline, was born there. I don't know how long we lived here. I do remember Hershel and I playing in a very picturesque place. Beautiful ravine to play in and around. We had hens that would hide their nests. I recall finding some hens' nests full of eggs and taking them to Mom.

4. Dad moved back down the road about three miles to what was known as the Rho Cox house. My dad owned the place at this time. This house was larger, had a good smokehouse and no well. We had to carry water from a spring for

everything. Hershel, Elsie, and I carried little buckets, but we did help. We lived here about three years.

a. It was here that the triplet babies were born on September 9, 1928. This made Mom have six babies in three years. The babies were named R.D., J.C., and L.V.

b. This house had a long porch across the front, and it was high off the ground. She had an old rocking chair that she said, "It not only rocked, but it walked, too." Mom said, "Many a time she'd be out on the porch rocking two babies at a time and go to sleep and would wake up to find she was on the very edge of the porch." Wasn't God good to her?

c. Mom and Dad were invited to bring the babies to the Nacogdoches County Fair that fall. People gave the babies some money. I enjoyed picking up little ice cream spoons.

d. The babies took diarrhea. Dad had the doctors come several times, but they didn't know how to treat it. R.D. died at six months of age. L.V. died as a crawling baby at ten months. J.C. died five days later. I remember this and about the babies crawling.

e. The next set of twins were born here on May 25, 1930. Laura Mae and James Ray: one was still born and the other one died the next day. I'm not sure which. These two babies were buried in the same coffin. All of these babies are buried at Melrose.

Can you imagine such heartache that Mom and Dad and family must have suffered? They surely looked to the Lord. At my age and at this time, I distinctly remember praying for Mom and Dad. They put us children out in the smokehouse when the babies were so sick or dying.

5. We moved here to a place called the "Red Land Place". It was just that. This place belonged to Grandpa Lee. We moved in 1931 here. I do not know this to be a fact, but I feel sure that Dad had to sell the Rho Cox place that we moved from. We loved this new place, but it was a long way to walk to school; three miles each way. It only seems like yesterday that Dad scooped us up in the middle of the night and took us to Grandma Lee. The stork was coming again. I remember Dad asking Grandpa for $20.00. Grandpa said, "Look in my britches pocket and get it." Dad had to go to Nacogdoches to get the doctor and return with him.

   a. Laverne did not wait for the doctor and Dad. She got there before they did. Aunt Pearl was with Mom. This date was October 26, 1931. We were so tickled to have a new sister. We had diphtheria when we lived here.

6. The next move was a very happy time. We moved back to the main road in 1932. We would only have to walk a half mile to school. We could even come home for lunch. This was during the depression and things were bad. I never remember us not having plenty to eat.

   a. There was a big fruit orchard at this place and a good deep well right in the yard. Dad worked on WPA about this time. Also, he peddled groceries all over the county. Many times, the roads would be so bad, he'd spend the night with someone. He farmed his land and raised his feed, corn, and maize every place we lived. We always had cows, pigs, chickens, a milk cow, and a garden.

b. We lived here when Mom and all of us children had the measles. She lost a baby here due to the measles. Then in August of 1934, Faye was born at this house. Faye was my pride and joy. I helped Mom with her all the time when she was little.

c. We lived here when Grandpa Lee's barn and animals burned.

d. We lived here when G.Y. Fleniken killed himself. I can't remember for sure, but I believe he jumped into a well. He was 22 years of age. The school turned out and everybody walked to his funeral. My, My, how every sad. Some of his relatives actually tried to jump into the hole after they had let him down, probably his mother. This really scared me bad. I dreamed about him every night for months. Then my Grandma Lee died. I did not want to go see her dead, but I did, and it didn't affect me like that. It had rained all night before her death and washed the road out at the bottom of the schoolhouse hill. They had her funeral at home and only a few went to the cemetery. They buried her at Cove Springs. Grandma Lee was born November 14, 1873, and died May 4, 1934, at age 62 years.

e. Last, but not least, Bro. Mott an old Pentecostal preacher had been coming to Jamesville three or four years preaching the Holy Ghost and many of my relatives received the Holy Ghost, including Grandma Lee.

7. In 1936, we moved to Oak Ridge because of the school. We had gone to Jamesville as long as we could go there.

a. Dad had a shop and did mechanic work. Every time Dad would have to run to town to buy a car part.

Some of us kids would want to go, especially Hershel. Mom told us one day "it's not that he doesn't want you all to go, but you'll have to keep yourselves clean and your hair combed, and he would let you go." I seem to remember it worked. Dad must not have made his fortune there because we only lived there one year.

b. Mom had a store in a big room of the home and sold groceries, etc. Mom was sick with 'spells'. We could not determine what was wrong. Many nights neighbors and family would sit up all night with her and continually put hot poultices on her stomach. Years later, she found a doctor who determined that she had a hernia on both sides. Surgery fixed that.

8. In 1937 we moved to a little house near the creek below where Fee Gartman owns now. The very day we moved; Faye ate some berries that were poison. They made her very sick.

a. We lived here when Uncle Willie and his family came to go work with us in Mr. Roy Atkinson's field. We had already left to go and met them. They had not eaten breakfast, so we turned around and went back with them. Mom was not expecting them, so she said, "Well, we'll have something." She made lots more hot biscuits and had plenty of butter. She opened several quarts of canned berries and sweetened them good. They ate like it was good. Mom was embarrassed that she didn't have more.

b. This was the first year that Dad heard about pulling cotton in West Texas, so we went.

c. Dad had an old Packard car which was pretty nice and awful big. There were seven of us and two more grown boys went along with us. Dad put cotton sacks filled with clothing on the running boards. He put mattresses on top of the car and a big old trunk full of everything. He probably went every bit of 35 miles an hour. The roads were not all that good. We stayed two nights at roadside parks before we got to where we were going. We probably stopped at Ralls, Texas that year. This was to be a practice about every year after that.

9. The next year, 1938, we had only a few hundred yards to move. This house was directly in front of the Fee Gartman house. I believe Jewel Atkinson owned this land and house. It was good farming land.

10. In 1940, Dad rented land from Mr. Horace Matteauer, a blind man. This was a very good man to work for. He had good, rich, bottom land. Dad made some good crops. We lived here for two years. Jesse made his appearance here on a stormy day. There was a Gulf storm on, and it was bad weather. Jesse was born August 8, 1940. It was here that we lived when I began to hear about Cecil (my to-be husband) from his sister, Marie.

   a. I had wanted the Holy Ghost so bad, but I wanted to be sure it would be alright with my dad to be baptized so I wrote him a letter. He was working at Freeport. He wrote back and told me "Whatever I wanted to do about living for the Lord was alright with him." I do not remember who baptized me.

   b. Mom received the Holy Ghost when we lived here too, but she did not tell anyone for several years. She finally did and was baptized in Jesus Name.

   c. I spent many, many hours in prayer when I lived here. I'd go down in the pasture under a certain tree to pray. Then one place there was a big, big round bale of hay that I prayed beside.

d. There were no churches anywhere closer than Nacogdoches. I would go across the road and pray with Sister Allie Gregston (a blind lady) which was Brother Freeman Bryant's sister.

e. Brother Barron begin to come to Chireno about 1937 to preach brush arbor meetings. Then he came to homes for one-night services. About 1940 someone came close to our home and had an open-air meeting. I went each night. Sister Donahoe probably came to this meeting. I know her sister-in-law Mildred Pate attended. She prayed with me, and I loved her.

f. We lived here when I got my first love letter from Cecil. Many more were to follow the next two years. He had volunteered for the army to keep from being drafted.

11. In 1941, we moved to Herty, TX, a small community on 103 near Lufkin. The paper mill is there. Dad went there to haul logs, I believe, or pulp wood to the paper mill.

a. This was quite an experience for us children. The first day of school, we had learned that LaVerne and LaFaye were to go to Moffett, but we had to go to Lufkin High School.

b. We went to Lufkin and saw that big school. It scared us awful bad. Hershel would not even go in. He stayed outside all day. We missed the bus, but Hershel walked home with us. We did not tell Mom and Dad at the time. Elsie and I went back the next day because we had registered, and we missed the bus again. Our teacher took us home and he saw where we lived and told us we were in the Moffett District; therefore, we could go to Moffett. I believe we walked to Moffett also.

c. It was at the time I was awful sick again. I took with a hard chill and was out of it for several days. Dad had a doctor twice, I believe, he said I had pneumonia. I had gotten some better and Jesse was very sick with his ears. Mom was up cooking breakfast and getting Dad off to work. She called and asked me if I felt like getting up and holding him. She took a chair up to the fireplace and brought him and put him in my lap. She told me not to get up with him. He went to sleep, and I felt so bad, I did get up and dropped him in the hearth of the fireplace. It didn't hurt him as much as it did me. I was 16 years old then.

12. I believe we moved to Easy Street in Chireno for the next year. I believe Dad was waiting to move into the big house of Mr. Horace Matteauer's. I remember one day; Dr. Taylor Mast was down there for some reason and Mom told him Jessee would eat sand when he was playing. Dr. Taylor said, "It won't hurt him. Don't you know chickens eat sand?" We only lived here part of the year 1942.

13. We moved to the big house of Mr. Horace Matteauer in 1942. Many eventful things took place here. Brother Barron started coming down there and preaching around in the community. A Sister Blackman from Cisco, Texas came to the community and held a revival. She stayed with us.

14. In 1943, we moved to Camp Chemical near Freeport. The war was on, and everybody went to work in the defense plants.

a. Hershel, Elsie, and I did not return to school, something I've always regretted. I loved school and should have gone back, even after Cecil's death.

b. We went to work at a big cafeteria at Camp Chemical. This place was huge and booming, not only with defense workers but there was a big army camp there, too, that's why they called it Camp Chemical. My job here was to fix lunches for people to pick up and take to work with them. I went to work at 6:00 a.m.

c. After the men picked up the lunches, I started preparing sandwiches and salads. I also carried cold drinks, coffee, and milk. I had a small building down inside the rubber plant where I went about 11:00 a.m. and stayed until about 1:00 p.m. I couldn't drive but a boy who worked there took the food and drinks in a van for me. Sometimes I rode, sometimes I walked. I sold this during the noon hours. I carried my Bible with me and read it if I wasn't busy. I was sixteen years of age.

d. Selvia came to live with us while we were living at Camp Chemical. She worked at the cafeteria longer than I did. I came home and got married.

e. Dad had worked hard at the defense plant and Elsie, and I had too. We gave Dad all our pay checks except $5 or $10 a week. He was saving to buy a farm from Mr. Jim Still at the Attoyac River.

f. I was with Dad when we went to Mr. Jim Still's house and paid $50.00 which was earnest money on the farm. He had a couple of months to bring back the first payment of $500.00 more. Then he paid the farm note on a yearly basis of $200.00 per year.

69

g. There was a pretty good old house on the farm but some other renters who were farming the land needed a few months to find another place. So, we knew we were going to live in the 'Little Red House' as we called it.

h. We left Freeport on March 7, 1943, coming to a place of our own. The weather was bad, lightning and raining most of the way. By the time we got to the little house, it was very cold, no heat, no lights, no ceiling in the house. We finally got beds and covers to lay down a while and try to get warm. It was way over in the night. Dad did find some wood and made a fire in the old mud fireplace. This house had three rooms: two bedrooms and a kitchen.

i. We learned the next day that it had come a bad tornado in San Augustine that night.

j. Early the next morning, Dad took his gun and went hunting and killed a big fat duck. Mom made duck and dressing for lunch. Selvia still talks of how good it was.

k. This place at the river had two more houses on it at this time. One was hardly livable. It was a log house that set up the road a short distance from the big house and across to the right coming out.

l. Then another house set up the road a short distance on the left side. Several of the relatives lived there: Uncle Carter and Aunt Vernice and family. Cecil and I lived there when Charles started walking. Also, Clifford Pinkston got killed when we lived there.

m. Dad moved to the other house the next year. However, the house that is there now, Dad built himself, along with family members. I don't exactly remember the year.

BED BUG ITEM

And there were bedbugs. I remember every time we moved, Dad filled the wash pot and fired it, having boiling water for Mom's use. She scalded the walls, floors, and bedsprings.

Even then, sometimes she would find a bedbug on her mattress. She had a little oil can with a long spout on it. She kept kerosene oil in it to disinfect when she found any sign of a bedbug. Keep in mind, back then there were no sprays. Many people had straw beds, but we always had cotton mattresses.

DIPPING THE COWS

Years ago, there was no way to kill the lice and ticks off the cows except to dip them in big, long, vats with lots of creosote in the vats. On these particular days, it was fun to see all the farmers driving their cattle to the vats. Then on the way back, there would be lots of cows bawling.

NO REFRIGERATORS

Mom kept her sweet milk in a bucket with a lid on it and then placed it in a big, long container and let it down into the well or spring. Also, she kept her butter the same way.

Mom said she had put her cold corn bread in a syrup bucket with a tight lid on it and hung it on a nail in the house to keep ants and flies off it many times.

NO IRONING BOARDS OR ELECTRIC IRONS

We used a flat iron and heated it on the stove or at the fireplace hearth. I have ironed many times on a table, with a quilt over the table. Then later we used a nice, covered board and put that across the backs of two chairs.

SELLING BLACKBERRIES

We older children picked berries and sold them to our neighbors. I believe we used syrup buckets to pick them in and sold them for 10 cents a bucket.

BAD TRIP HOME FROM WEST TEXAS BEFORE MARRIAGE

Dad again had taken his family to West Texas to pull cotton. This was the year of 1941. We were at Ralls, Texas working for a Mr. Curtis Richards. The weather was getting very, very bad and the cotton was about gathered. Dad came in and told Mom, "Get packed. We are going home." Dad put a tarp over his truck, and I believe that Uncle Hebron and some of his family were coming back with us in the truck.

We didn't get very far until the rain turned into ice and the truck quit running. The Lord was with us and let us be in front of a farmhouse. Dad went across the highway and asked if we could spend the night. The man told him, "I have plenty of wood to keep a fire going but not enough beds." Most everyone sat up all night. We could not have slept if we'd had a chance because of the children. I believe it was Laverne who cried all night with the earache.

The water in the gas lines had frozen. Things were iced over the next morning. Dad got the truck going the next day. This was December 7, 1941, the day Pearl Harbor was bombed.

WAGON TRIP TO GRANDMA HOOPER'S

I don't remember if this was a necessity or if Dad just wanted to take us children on a trip in the wagon. This was quite a trip from Jamesville to Aiken. I'm not sure the distance.

I do remember Dad driving down into the edge of a pond and letting the horses get a drink. It seemed that those horses had to pull hard going up the hills. You must remember these roads were not paved and the ruts sometimes were deep or the sandy places affording lots of grit and grime on the way.

My Dad and Mom knew everybody at most houses. Dad often stopped to talk to friends. There was a man that lived toward Aiken that raised big hogs. I mean big, big hogs. I have a picture of one of these hogs he raised and when he butchered it, the hog weighed 625 pounds. 1927 was the year. Elsie and I both remember seeing one of these big hogs that he raised so evidently, he raised another one because we were too young to remember in 1927.

We children really enjoyed going to Grandma and Grandpa Hooper's in a wagon. Grandpa always met us at the gate and kissed all of us except Dad. We never tired of talking. You could see more traveling on a wagon than you could a car; birds, rabbits, snakes, flowers, dogs and all the other children out playing.

MAKING GOVERNMENT MATTRESSES (BEFORE MARRIAGE)

This was in 1941, I believe. It would have been in the summertime. The government gave people cotton and ticking material and had a designated place to make the mattresses. They also had someone to show us how to make them. This was at Moffett. We were going to school there at the time.

This particular day, I was coming home with Aunt Ella and Uncle Covy from making the mattresses. We stopped at a lady's house to buy some yard eggs. They told me to go to the door and buy them. As I neared the fence, this huge bulldog jumped up and started toward me. Before I knew it, I had called that dog an ugly name and Uncle Covy and Aunt Ella laughed at me They were surprised, and I was ashamed.

PLAY PARTIES

When I was growing up, most people had no cars. There was no electricity. Not much to do for amusements. There were two forms of entertainment that were quite popular. The play parties and square dance. Let me say, that I only went to one dance in my life. It was at Uncle Willie and Aunt Pearline Hooper's. I did not dance. More of a family affair, however they did have music, which we didn't have at the play parties. We only sung and did our thing by the singing.

There were several songs that Mom tried to teach us. One of the songs was Skip to My Lou. Another song was The Girl I Left Behind Me. Some of the words to this was:

On to the next and balance four

And bow to them so kindly

Oh, swing that girl, that pretty, little girl

Oh, the girl I left behind me.

First gent swing his opposite lady

Swing her by the right hand

Swing your partner by the left,

And promenade the girl behind you.

Oh, the girl, the girl, that pretty, little girl,

The girl I left behind me.

These parties were before I received the Holy Ghost. There had to be a leader who could call this in order for everyone else to follow. This may sound bad, but in reality, it was a clean game. We had these at our house or at the Layton's primarily. Our parties were adult supervised.

THE OLD OAK TREE

Down on the far, near the Attoyac River, stands a huge oak tree. I do not know how old this tree is, but it stands there unshakeable, unmovable thus far. A shelter in the storm and a shade in the heat. Many people have lived at this home site, but Mom probably lived there the longest, 42 years. This tree is a haven for the squirrels, crow, and any and all kinds of birds.

It has been used to just sit out under its wonderful shade for cool and comfort. Watch the cars pass by, going to the river. Uncle Noah sat there many, many hours of the day. Years ago, in fact, not until about 1947, did Dad get electricity at the farm. The shade was used to place a cot so Dad could lay down when he wasn't feeling well, or just to rest his weary bones as he rested from field work.

Children played under this tree. All of us children, our children, and grandchildren. During the summer harvest, the tree had tables nestled beneath it. These tables held corn, peas, tomatoes, squash, and cucumbers. We shelled peas, prepared our vegetables outside most all the time. All the goodies going into the freezer or canning jars, preparing for winter.

This old tree has seen many happy memories; people making ice cream, picnic, playing dominoes. Even sometimes a horse or a little calf could be found tied to the tree, eating some good green grass. Come fall, my, my, at the leaves that tree afforded. Mom always said the tree never shed the last leaf until new ones were budding out. Even the leaves were a fun thing for children to play in. They didn't mind doing a little raking of the leaves into a big pile, just to get to play in them.

Dad always had at least one dog. It usually could be found under the tree on hot weather. It would not be the same at the old home place without that tree.

DID YOU KNOW?

Hershel worked (plowed) all day for 75 cents for Mr. Willie Matteauer in 1942.

School teachers use to have to stay away from home in order to teach. They sometimes had to sleep on the porch on a cot. Therefore, they had to go to bed after everyone else did and get up before everyone got up.

Old timers made bread yeast with peach tree leaves and hops.

People referred to the article with the handle that you put under the bed at night as the 'vessel'.

When we had to go to the outhouse before indoor plumbing, we said we had to go see "Miz Jones".

It was forbidden to say boar, jackass, or bull. We said male hog, jack, and male cow. We referred to a female dog as a girl dog or lady.

No nice person said 'guts' in company.

It wasn't considered good taste to refer to a lady's leg. You said 'limb'.

Men always put their shirt tail inside. A teacher would say, "Johnnie, your shirt is blousing too much."

Long ago, people did not have bed springs. They only used rope tied crisscrossed on the bedstead and put a straw mattress on that.

People have used cow chips or buffalo chips for wood to cook their food.

When pioneers traveled and when it rained, cooking had to be done under the wagon or else inside the wagons.

People made their homes from logs and rough plain 1"x6". Then they put a strip of 1"x4" rough board outside to cover up the cracks. No such things as ceilings overhead. The walls were single. They made their shingles to go on top of the house. Many years ago, they did not use nails. They notched their timbers to fit together. Many old homes were built on a rock foundation.

The old log house that used to be on Dad's place was built with square nails. I'm pretty sure that I have one or two.

Long ago, people had to build their hog pens bear-proof, meaning they must have a top on the hog pens.

Indians stole people's meat and lard from their smokehouses, but the white people were willing to let them have that rather than be killed, which oftentimes they did murder for food.

People made chimneys out of different things. If they had nothing else, they used straw and mud. Then sometimes, they used rocks and mud to make them. This was before bricks. This mud was likened to our cement today. Something to hold them together. Some old folks used the chaff from wheat, rye, or barley, adding the red clay mud.

There were no hampers a long time ago. They made their own out of white Oak splits. They made the splits and made clothes hampers and baskets to carry corn, food, seed, peanuts, grain, or anything else. I have a couple of these old baskets.

Old timers made their chairs, tables, and cabinets. They called them 'safes'. This was a necessity to put food and dishes in.

The early settlers brought no bed springs or mattresses as they traveled. Mom said everyone spoke of going West. They traveled in covered wagons and usually in a caravan because of Indians and other hardships. There was a sort of security in numbers.

To make their mattresses, they used straw or feathers. They put these into a bed size cloth sack. If these beds were properly sunned and beat, they lasted many, many years. We never had either, I don't think, but the grandparents did. I didn't like to sleep on a feather bed. They raised their own ducks or chickens to make their beds and pillows. It took a long time to get enough to make one.

Many old timers never saw a mattress until they were grown. There were no bedsprings. The beds had rope bottoms. There were holes in the wooden sides and ends and they were laced back and forth. Grandma Hooper had such a bed. These ropes were taken out each year and washed, dried, and put back in.

My mother made lye soap. In fact, LaVerne, my sister, loves to make lye soap. Mom made it out of necessity. We washed clothes with it for many, many years. I remember when Oxydol came out. Mom was so happy. I'm not going to try and explain how to make lye soap. It's quite complicated to me.

Although we had a good cook stove, the kind that burned if you forever put stove wood into it. These stoves really cooked good food inside and on top of the stove also. When the weather was cold and bad or some of the family was sick, Mom would be the one to go into the kitchen and get the food to prepare on the fireplace. This was the only room with heat in it. She raked red hot coals out onto the hearth, which was the floor of the fireplace. This was where she boiled or fried our food. She used iron pots and pans with lids.

Some people made hominy in the wash pot. Mom made it many times, cooking it on the hearth of the fireplace. It was delicious.

Then there were ways and means to dry many foods, fruits, and vegetables. I've seen my grandmother gather her peaches to prepare them for drying. She put them on a pan or board and took them outside and put them on top of a low shed. She had to put something over the top and watch that a shower didn't come up. She turned these religiously and it took days to dry them.

The vegetables I've known of being dried were pumpkin, sweet potatoes, corn, okra, peas, and string beans.

Burying was another way of preserving food. They dug a trench on a sloping plot of ground and pulled up the cabbage, roots, and all, and buried them. They were covered with straw and then dirt. They kept most all winter. Irish potatoes were buried in this same manner. Usually, people made cellars to put sweet potatoes and their root vegetables into.

To keep their pork sausage from hog killing time in the fall through the winter months, people would make their pork sausage into patties and fry them. Then put them into a big mouth stone crock. This was like a 5-gallon vessel. They put a layer of sausage and then poured the hot grease over top, on and on this way until it was full. Then Grandma would tie a big, doubled flour sack over the top. These kept all winter.

As far as I remember, my grandma always had glass jars to can fruit and vegetables in. My Grandma Hooper canned everything. Grandpa ran a store, so she had access to her canning needs, and she canned jelly, preserves, fruits, vegetables, and pickles of all sorts. It was so much fun to go to her smokehouse and see all her canned stuff. Let me say here that Selvia's mom lived with my grandparents and Aunt Pearl did most of the work, I think. Selvia said one year she counted 400 jars of jams and jellies in the smoke house.

Dad raised his own hogs. He kept them penned and fed them until early spring, then he turned them out to run into the bottom where they ate acorns, nuts, and roots. Then when it came a big frost and stayed cold a night or two, Dad would go to the bottom and drive up the hogs. They would be fine and fat. This was a big day, exciting and lots of hard work for everyone big enough to work. Sometimes some of these hogs were put back in pens to feed awhile longer. The hogs were shot, bled, and then put into a big washpot and turned over and over to scald good. Then they were lifted out and put on a sheet of tin and covered with several burlap sacks that had been dipped in the boiling water. Then, in a short time, the sacks were lifted off and then the scraping of the hog to remove the hair. Then after the hog is clean of its hair, the hamstrings were exposed on both hind legs and a stout stick put through the hamstrings. The hog was hung up on a high pole and then the hog was gutted. They had a clean tub to catch the intestines. The liver was all that Dad kept that was inside the hog. He cut the gall bladder from the liver, and someone had a bowl ready to catch the liver. Sometimes, we took the leaf lard from off the intestines if Mom wanted to make the lye soap. Then there was a table to lay the hog carcass on and clean, hot water was poured all over the hog, inside and out. There would be a pan for the ribs, sausage pan, pan for the fat to be used to render for lard. Most every night of hog killing, we had tenderloin and pork ribs, along with Mom's good hot biscuits. Then there was quite a bit of meat to be smoked in the smokehouse. There were the shoulders, hams, what was called the side meat or what they make the bacon from. Sometimes, people canned some of the ribs like I have described previously concerning canning sausage. Then my, those good back bones and oddly enough, I loved the pig tail boiled with the backbone. Sometimes these were canned. Oh, I forget the head. The jowls were cut from the head. Most of the time, we didn't prepare the head, but one year after I came back from Mississippi, Dad killed a hog and I made hog head cheese. It was good.

I remember when you began to find 'bolted meal' in the stores, Mama called it. She did not like it at all. She has been used to using the stone ground meal that was made from our own home-grown corn.

When cars first came out, there was no gas gauge on them. Dad had to stick a stick in the gas tank to measure the gas. You had to crank the car with a crank up at the front of the car. Sometimes, the thing would 'kick' and almost break Dad's arm.

Just about every time, especially in the winter, that we went somewhere, we would have a flat or get stuck. Dad did not have a jack. He would go out in the woods and cut a prize pole and get a big log and everyone but me (I was scared.) would get on the end of that pole. That would pick up the car or pickup. Sometimes Dad made me help too by sitting on that prize pole.

We hear a lot now-a-days about water conservation but I'm here to tell you that I lived when we were aware of conserving every drop of water. We either carried water from a spring or had to draw it from a well for all my life until we bought the place on Looneville Road after I was married. We had no city water when we bought the place, but Cecil put a well pump in our well and, presto, we had to turn on the faucet. This was in 1948. Prior to this, we used the dish water to wash dishes, then we used it again to put 'shorts' (hog food) in the dish water and feed the hogs. We used bath water to either water the flowers or scrub the floors.

There were no washing machines when I was little. At least, I don't guess there were. We could not use them because of no electricity. I got my first washing machine when Edward was a baby. It was a wringer washer, that's what I wanted. This was 1950. Prior to that, before marriage, we carried water from a spring, rubbed our clothing on a rub board, boiled the white clothing in a wash pot, then rinsed them through about three tubs of rinse water, and then wrung them out by hand from each tub, then carried them to a line and hung them out.

There was no such thing as anti-freeze. Everyone had to drain the radiator every night when they thought there was danger of a freeze. I remember so many mornings, Dad would heat a tea kettle of warm water to put in his radiator first, then draw his water from the well to fill up his radiator.

I remember when the hogs squealed under the house. Mom and Dad said they were 'pulling for cover' meaning they were cold. This was very disruptive to your sleep.

There was sometimes when we had to grease the bread pan with a piece of meat rind.

During the war, we used food stamps for gasoline, sugar, and I believe, meat. We could not buy tires. Finally, they started making synthetic tires. After the war, margarine became available for the first time. It was white with a packet of food coloring to add to it. It came in a one-pound block, no sticks.

Most of the time as we grew up, we had no toothpaste, but when we did, Mom would continually tell us to just use a little bit about the size of a pea. We used a little clean cloth since we had no toothbrushes. All the other times, we used baking soda to brush our teeth.

In 1918, the Daily Sentinel cost 50 cents a month or the Weekly Sentinel cost $50 for one year. I have a receipt to this effect. Grandpa Lee paid for one year; $100, I'm assuming for the Weekly and the Daily.

In 1942, my Grandpa Hooper got a raise on his 'old age assistance' from $11 per month to $17 per month.

We raised our own popcorn, shelled it and my, was it so good when popped on the fireplace or stove.

Before 1945: There was no F.M. radio, no televisions, no frozen foods, plastic, no xerox machines, saying nothing about computers and all those things. No credit cards, dishwashers, clothes dryers, electric blankets, air conditioners, or drip-dry clothes. No instant coffee, cocoa, noodles, and milk. We didn't need this. We didn't even have a microwave oven, ha-ha.

A circus came to town and, as soon as the show was over and the people and animals gone, this man came across a man scooping up the horse manure. He looked up at the man and replied, "Boy! This ought a make tomatoes grow big!"

People used to have wall-to-wall beds instead of wall-to-wall carpet.

In 1939, a young girl would work every evening after school and on Saturdays for $3 a week and was happy to have the job.

Dressing for school in the wintertime was unpleasant to say the least. We dressed, bathed, combed our hair, and ate our breakfast by the fireplace. We only had one brother at this time. I guess he waited for us girls to get dressed and then came in and did accordingly.

DISOBEDIENCE AGAIN

When we lived at Oak Ridge, we went to Nacogdoches High School for some purpose concerning the school. Dad and Mom didn't too much like the idea to begin with but, with lots of persuasion, they let Elsie and I go. They told us be sure and stay at the school, but after we were through with the school business, we noticed a city bus coming by every once in a while, so we decided it would be nice to just ride all over town and back to the school. That's exactly what we did and lived with a guilty conscience about it. We did not tell them.

OLD SIGNS AND SAYINGS

Cross your broom and mop at the back door. It scares off evil spirits.

Any symbol or sign of the cross holds powerful magic.

When you nail up a horseshoe over your door, put the open end up, so your fortune won't spill out.

Tis said a lone tree draws lightning, especially a walnut tree. Never stand in an open door nor underneath a lone tree or near a bob-wire fence. Lightning may strike.

A whistling girl and a crowing hen always come to some bad end.

Don't kick the fellow responsible for your problems. If you should, the chances are you couldn't sit down for several days.

People can have a great imagination and be sharp as a tack but be short on horse sense.

Even if you cannot be a lighthouse, you can be a candle.

Angry words... like chickens... come home to roost.

There's only one animal on earth that has four knees. It is an elephant.

The true lady does not giggle constantly at every little thing that's said.

A woman usually is more religiously inclined.

A woman is more honest than a man, our prisons and jails prove this.

The mother is the angel spirit of the home.

Just one sentence of encouragement or praise is a joy for a day.

You can wound a child for life if you talk harsh to your children. Speak soberly and quietly reprove; best done in private.

Children will not trouble you long. They grow up. Nothing on Earth grows as fast as children.

A belief grew up that if a young girl slept under a new quilt, she would dream of the boy she was going to marry. Was that true? I'm sure I don't know.

We become friends with life when we become friends with Jesus.

With every privilege, there comes a responsibility.

Patience is not to be thought in the sense of sitting down and hearing things and just simply bowing the head and letting the tide of events flow over you, but rather the ability in bearing things to turn them into something worthwhile.

What we see depends on which way we look. 'Two prisoners were looking through the bars. One saw all the mud on the ground, the other saw the stars.'

No man on Earth ever did anything without a vision. Things that are humanly impossible, become divinely possible.

There is a difference in going about doing good and just going about.

We often blame Satan for our misdeeds but much too often, some of our meanness is our own idea.

One who is well fed, warm, and in good health cannot understand one who is hungry, cold, and ill.

We cannot know comfort if we have never known pain.

Hardening of the heart ages more people than hardening of the arteries.

One sure sign of old age is when your broad mind and narrow waist begin to change places.

People of high intelligence talk about ideas. People of average intelligence talk about things. People with no intelligence talk about other people. Where are we in this lineup?

If you can't help worrying, remember that worrying can't help you either!

The flower of prayer needs watering three times a day!

If you want people to see what Jesus can do for them, let them see what Jesus has done for you!

If you meet someone without a smile, give them one of yours!

Steady nerves and a quiet mind are not things we go out and find; they are things we create.

People who have no time, don't think. The more you think, the more time you have.

Responsibility alone drives man to toil and brings out his best gifts and qualities.

You fulfill the promise that lies latent within you by keeping your promises to yourself.

Self-confidence carries conviction; it makes other people believe in us.

The smallest error should humble us, but we should never permit the greatest to discourage us.

Fame is a vapor, popularity an accident, and riches fly away. Those who love us today will hate us tomorrow. Our character and our Lord Jesus Christ will endure forever.

Getting angry is easy. Keeping your wits and staying calm isn't.

LIVE ONE DAY AT A TIME

A wise man pointed to the traffic flowing over the bridge and said to his troubled friend, "See how much weight that bridge carries in a day, a week, a month, or a year? How? By taking only a few cars at a time! It would collapse if it didn't carefully ration its load.

You'll find enormous peace of mind when you space your worries and learn to trust God and live one day at a time!

Space your worries. Ask yourself, "What should I concern myself with today?" Then tackle that concern with all you've got! So don't be anxious about tomorrow. God will take care of your tomorrow, too. Live one day at a time! Matthew 6:34

COFFINS AND BURIAL PREPARATIONS

Coffins were often times made at home, especially for a baby or an infant. Mr. Eric Green at Chireno, who ran a service station, also sold coffins, which he kept upstairs. Coffins long ago were made wide at the top or head and narrowed almost to a point on the end. The lids were not hinged on but were padded good and just fit and were laid on top.

Both my Granddaddy and Grandmother Hooper's bodies were not carried to a funeral home. They were not embalmed. They were bathed, clothed, and prepared for burial at home and went from there to the cemetery. My Grandmother Lee's body was done the same way, no embalming, prepared at home for her burial.

DAD PRAYS FOR RAIN

One year, Dad and Mom had the land rented on Highway 21, near Mr. Glen Matteauer's house. Dad had lots of produce planted over there, but he also had a big field of watermelons growing. Summer months were so hot and dry. It just looked as if Dad was going to lose all his labor and money he had invested in that crop. He told Charles that he got down on his knees out in the middle of that watermelon field and prayed that God would send his fields rain.

Can you believe that God did send a really good rain on Dad's crop, but the mysterious thing about it was, that it only rained on his fields and not on either side.

Yes, we do believe this because Dad told the truth, but mostly because he was asking Jesus and believing in His divine providence. Dad made a fabulous crop of watermelons and produce. They had a fruit stand there on the highway.

AS A CHILD, OUR FAMILY HAD 'THE ITCH'

Yes, Sir, we sure did contract this pesky little freeloader we called 'the itch'. I wonder how many would admit hosting a siege of it. In the small school we attended, it was very common for a child to have 'the itch'. I don't ever remember us contracting this nuisance but one time. It was highly contagious, but unlike measles or mumps, one bout with 'the itch' did not produce immunity.

Having 'the itch' was bad enough, but not as bad as the Sulphur and grease Mom rubbed all over us. I know Mom was careful to send us to school clean, but I don't see how our teacher could endure all the children and their various kinds of scents. Sometimes people would burn their night clothes and sheets after this treatment of Sulphur and grease.

A FUNERAL I ATTENDED AT AGE 9

This was the first funeral I remember attending. It was so very sad. This young man was only 22 years old at the time of his death. He took his own life. I'm not even sure how he committed suicide. His family took this terrible. One person tried to jump in the grave as they were lowering the coffin. The school that I attended turned out school and everyone walked and went to the funeral. He is buried at Cove Springs.

This dealt me such a blow that I dreamed about him nearly every night. My Grandmother Lee was very bad sick during this time and when she died, I said, "I'm not going to her funeral." Mom told me, "Yes, you are. This will not be like J. Y's funeral. It was then that I realized that living for God was important. I had no bad dreams about my Grandma Lee.

MR. LOUIS TAYLOR

This man and wife were our close neighbors. They had two children, Leon and Ealine. The girl died after she was grown. I'm not sure if this is correct, but according to my memory, Mr. Louis got up one cold morning and took a cold shower and it killed him. He was only 48 years of age at his death.

THE WHOLE HOUSE

Some said it was a great equalizer between the poor and the rich. Whatever, it was a most necessary house. There was a well-worn path to the outhouse. Most all of these houses were small, weather-beaten, and certainly were not visited more often than necessary. It was most dreaded on a cold, dark night. I was always afraid of a snake or spiders. Usually someone would go with you at night, to scare the boogers away, or anyway, to be moral support.

We had a good 'outhouse', by that I mean, it had been built by burying two or three big concrete culverts. We didn't have to move ours as some people did. In fact, I'm not sure if it's still there at the farm or not. It was there when Mom and I moved to Nacogdoches. Oh, yes! They had an inside bathroom for many, many years, but Dad liked to go to the outhouse occasionally. Years ago, there was no Charmin, there was just a Sears catalog.

MAKING RIBBON CANE SYRUP

As I was growing up, my dad and Granddaddy Lee raised sugar cane by the field full. Each fall, this meant syrup making time. I recall Mom making supper for the works and Hershel, Elsie, and I would carry it to the syrup mill. This would be after dark, and we walked about one and a half miles. Hershel and I were about 8 or 9 years old.

When they started cooking off a batch, they had to stay with it. They had to watch it very closely, keeping it stirred most of the time. I'm going to try and tell you children somewhat of how this procedure went.

There was an apparatus that someone fed the cane into. There was a long pole on top of this and there was a horse that went around and around, thus pressing the juice out of the cane stalks. I'm assuming there were some big rollers that went together and caused the juice to be extracted. Later years, I believe they used a tractor instead of the horse for the pulling power.

The juice from the stalks ran down a wooden trough and dripped through a cloth fastened over the top of a big barrel. Buckets of this thin, green juice were emptied into one end of the long evaporator. Many people liked to drink this cane juice, but I did not like it. Anyone could hardly believe that the green foamy stuff that looked like scum from a pond could turn into pretty, golden, delicious syrup.

The evaporator was divided into several sections. It was fixed to allow the juice, as it got thick, to flow from one section into the next, until it finally got to the last one, and this was the 'run off' section. They had either a plug to let the juice go from one section to the other or somehow raised the sheet metal to allow the syrup to keep traveling to its destination.

This big, long evaporator was made from sheet metal, I believe. It was built on high, steel legs. This was for two reasons. Firstly, so the ones who were stirring did not have to bend their backs. Secondly, there was a fire box under the evaporator. Long slabs of wood were fed into this big fire box. The ashes fell on the ground under this. They had a skirt of metal around the fire box to offer some protection from the heat. It also had a high flue on one end to make it have drawing power, similar to a stove pipe on a cook stove.

As the juice would thicken, it was moved to the next compartment through a small opening which was at the end of each section. It seemed that if the cane was really good and sweet, it took less time to 'cook off'. It took 50 gallons of juice to make one gallon of syrup.

They put a handful of baking soda in the juice after it started cooking down some. This helped the foam to collect so it could be skimmed off, somewhat like jelly. It took someone who really knew what they were doing to know precisely when the syrup was ready to be poured up. They took the plug up slowly and tested the syrup by seeing how it dropped. When it dropped one drop at a time, it seemed to be ready to 'run off'.

There was a wooden stopper, and it was pulled when the syrup was ready. There was a cloth strainer over their new syrup buckets which the syrup was poured into. I believe they had a small wooden trough that the syrup ran down and into a cloth-covered syrup bucket. The strained syrup was a very pretty, golden, clear color.

I don't recall how much trouble it was to work and raise a cane patch, but I recall how bad a job it was to cut the stalks at the bottom of the stalk, pile it, and then strip it. That meant, get the long shoot things off. I guess they may have been called leaves or fodder. Then it had to be loaded and taken to the syrup mill. Grandpa and Dad made syrup for other people in the community. They got a percentage of the syrup.

THINGS THE OLD MAN TAUGHT THE BOY

I read a book many years ago and copied these excerpts from the book.

Shoot quail one at a time, aim at one only.

A dog or a man has got to do what he has to do to earn his keep and he's got to do it right.

A fellow can learn a lot about living from watching his dog.

Any mistake you let your dog make is your fault.

A quail will walk off from where he roosted, but he likes to fly back home. It's a shame that a man can't take a hint from this.

When the old man handed his gun to his grandson, he told him, "Remember, you have my reputation in your hands now."

Don't cross a fence with a gun in your hands. Lay it 10 feet from where you will cross the fence.

Go with a boy all summer getting him accustomed to seeing things, instead of just telling him and him forgetting them.

A mama turtle digs a deep hole and lays her eggs in it, at a rate of about 6 per minute. She cries as she lays them. The male is smaller than the female and he never, ever comes out of the ocean. He lives there and they breed there.

Fishing is good for you. It gives a person time to collect his thoughts and rearrange them neat and in orderly fashion.

People who go out and fish, in a way, are heroes just because they have enough sense to loaf all day without people watching them.

Never be lazy in front of people. Loafing is fine, but energetic people get mad if you take it easy in front of them.

This old man said, "I don't admire people who are industrious all the time."

To cure the mange on your dog, use old oil from your car with Sulphur added. Rub this all over your dog.

Two wrongs never make a right.

A child is taught in his own backyard, so to speak, just as you teach a dog discipline, with a little switch.

Solitude can be really exciting if you play it right. Do what you like to do best sometimes, not what others expect of you.

Boys need more rest than adults do. Some deluded idea, that boys were created to run errands for the old folks.

For instance, boys aren't supposed to like white meat of a chicken; but rather just backs and wings and legs. Grown-ups are supposed to eat the white meat.

Boys are supposed to like to split kindling and clean fish and gut birds, run errands, rake yards, and cut grass. "Speaking as one who knows," the Old Man said, "I would like to say that the grown-up idea of what boys like is a sight different from what boys think boys like.

True, too true, and unjust, but the grown-up idea is that they are conditioning the boy for the toils and troubles of manhood.

There is no excuse for impoliteness; 'Sir' and 'Please' and 'Thank you, ma'am' are as cheap as dirt. Ordinary good manners are a measure of a man. Only a fool is rude when he doesn't have to be.

A real gentleman starts down at his boots and works up to his hat. A gentleman is, first of all, polite. A gentleman never talks down to anyone. A gentleman isn't greedy. A gentleman pays his score as he goes. He doesn't take what he can't put back, and if he borrows, he borrows from a bank. He never troubles his friends and relatives with his troubles.

A boy has to grow up to be a man someday. You can delay the process, but you can't protect the boy from manhood forever. The best and easiest way is to expose the boy to people who are already men; bad and good, drunk and sober, lazy and industrious. It is, after all, up to the boy when all is said and done. There are a lot of boys who never get to be men and a lot of men who never quit being boys.

Nobody ever got any younger because if they had, I would have heard about it and maybe bought some. So, what a man has to do is take a little time off as he grows older and devote the waste spaces to remembering the things he did, that he maybe won't every do again. When you get tired thinking about all the things you've done, you can always use the time thinking about what you'd like to do in the future. Have you done anything lately that you admired? In other words, use what God has given you when you are young, and then when you get old, you can still pray, talk on the phone, or reminiscence.

As I grow older, I believe more and more that no goodness or kindness is every truly lost.

Girls, always hold back a little with a boy. A boy will soon lose interest in a girl who is easy to get. A little mystery and reserve, that's what attracts a man most.

This was copied years ago. Author unknown.

FOOD FOR THOUGHT

I found this in Ma Lee's handwriting. I don't know if she wrote it or copied it.

We must be silent before we can listen.

We must listen before we can learn.

We must learn before we can prepare.

We must prepare before we can serve.

We must serve before we can lead.

The way to Heaven is to turn right and go straight.

OLD TIMEY RECIPES

Crock Grapes – collect dry fox grapes. Pack them in a churn and pour boiling hot, fresh molasses or syrup over them. Take two clean cloths. Dip the first one in hot beeswax and the second in hot tallow and tie each cloth separately around the top of the churn. Make this in the fall when grapes are in and are fresh and ripe. Then set the churn in a cool place until winter. These can be eaten in the winter after they are mildly fermented. You might not want to eat too much of this (ha, ha). This is just an old, old recipe. I'm sure people did make it and eat thereof.

Pear Preserves – Wash pears, peel, and cut into quarters. Rinse and place a layer of sugar and a layer of pears until all the fruit has been used. Let this stand overnight. Put over moderate heat and cook until well done and a syrup has been made from the mixture. Put into sterile jars and seal.

Buttermilk – You had to save a couple of milking's. Then Mom took the cream off each milking. Then she'd add this cream to a gallon of whole milk and leave the churn covered until it clabbered for a couple of days or more, depending on the weather. This church had a top with a wooden dasher in it. This you inserted in the churn, through the lid. Then you churn, churn, churn, hoping to make not only buttermilk, but butter. This was good stuff.

Fried Mush – They used home ground meal, stirring enough meal into a boiling kettle partially filled with 1/3 water, 2/3 pork or beef or chicken broth. Use the amount to fit your family. When the meal was very thick, it was poured into a loaf pan and let cool overnight. The next morning it was cut into thick slices, dredged in flour, and dropped into an iron skillet with hot oil and fried until brown, turning to brown on both sides. This was used when people did not have bacon and was quite filling and satisfying. I have eaten this myself.

Pear Do – Old timers believed "waste not, want not". They took their left-over cold biscuits and cold cornbread and made a pudding of a sort. They crumbled 4 cups corn bread and 2 cups crumbled biscuits, 1 large, chopped onion, dash of pepper, 1/3 cup melted butter or bacon grease, pinch of salt, sage to taste, hot milk to moisten, and 3 eggs. Mix all together, bake in a bread pan. This was a makeshift or substitute used in the days of the depression.

SCHOOL DAYS

The beginning of my going to school was at Jamesville, three miles east of Melrose. This building consisted of two rooms.

In the right-hand side, Mrs. Myrtie Austin taught the first, second, and third grades. I believe they let the children start at age five sometimes.

There was a big, long blackboard at the front side of the room. One day, several of the pupils were up there and the teacher was asking for our names. Mrs. Myrtie evidently had her head down and was checking each one off as we called our names. When it came my time, I answered by saying, "Me." She said, "Who is Me?" The laugh was on me.

Mrs. Myrtie had several low tables for the smaller children to sit and study. The older ones had desks. There was a raised platform in this room. Mrs. Myrtie's desk was on this platform. Each holiday, especially at Christmas, we had plays, programs, a large Christmas tree, and gifts for all. This was always a community affair. People came from all over the hills and valleys. Most people back then came in wagons or on horseback. A few people had cars.

We used a big, iron heater to heat the school. The larger boys from the other room usually brought our wood for our room on this side that housed the smaller children.

On the other side of the building was Mrs. Effie Fowler's room. She taught fourth, fifth, and sixth grades. This room also had a big, black heater in it. Our teachers built the fire, therefore they had to get there earlier than the students.

I remember the big maps on stands that Mrs. Fowler so aptly used in her teaching. This room was filled with school desks and the teacher's large desk. These rooms had big, high windows. We always found observances that called for decorating the windows.

Keep in mind, we had no electricity, no indoor bathrooms, and no running water. We had two nice outdoor toilets, one for the women and girls, one for the boys.

We had a big wooden barrel that was filled with water each morning. There was a dipper or cup for drinking. Oh yes, we all used the same dipper.

We had what we called a cloak room then, for the purpose of hanging our coats and hats, and placing our lunch buckets. Needless to say, if a child happened to get lice on their heads, someone else was likely to find one on themselves. Overall, though, I don't remember of many disturbances at this school.

We had volleyball nets and baseball games besides the other games I have mentioned on another page.

One very important thing was the day Mr. Bill Brown came by with his truck peddling groceries. Mrs. Myrtie would take us children out there on the road and buy us all something, candy, or gum.

Our teachers walked to school, just like we all did, most all the time. Mrs. Effie walked about two miles each way.

We strictly had school here at Jamesville. We were taught Reading, Writing, and Arithmetic. Then we had History and Geography. More importantly they taught us behavior, honesty, and courtesy.

There were play periods, at noon was the longest time for play. The boys loved to wrestle. I didn't like this at all. It was for fun.

We girls went across the road from the school and made us "playhouses" down on that big, tall pine thicket floor. We had a living room, with chairs and sofas made from pine straw. Then there were the bedrooms with large beds, some rooms had two beds. We made pillows for our beds. All this was pine straw. We must have a kitchen, so we had a kitchen too. We had a little brush broom and kept our little houses swept very clean. Sometimes we had some sort of a doll or a few little dishes to use. We spent many hours and had great fun in these make-believe houses.

The first year Hershel and I started to school, we had to walk three miles there and three miles back. Sometimes our shoes would get a hole in the bottom, and we'd put cardboard in them because of the frost biting our toes. I do think of how cold it was for us, but I was thankful then to go to school and I'm more thankful now that I had feet and legs to walk on.

MRS. EFFIE FOWLER

Mrs. Effie was not only our teacher in fourth and fifth grades, but also was our neighbor. When Hershel and I were about four years old, she kept begging Mom to let us go with her to school. Mom relented to us going, dressed us for the occasion, and she took us. I mean we walked with her about 1 ½ miles at least.

Hershel didn't stay very long, he left, and went to Grandpa and Grandma Lee's which was nearby. He climbed in the barn and stayed until school was out. I stayed a few hours longer, but I was worried about him, so I went outside and crawled under the schoolhouse (it was high off the ground) and cried until school was out. I'm sure she didn't want us to go again.

GAMES AND ENTERTAINMENT

For entertainment at home and school, we played Jacks. This was a little girl game. I was a whiz at this, could play several games, without missing a time. Boys played Marbles, for 'keeps', and sometimes it spelled trouble. They played Mumble Peg with their knives. Jumping the Rope game for boys and girls. We were usually barefoot. The adjustments of the rope only heightened the progression through 'high water', 'hot pepper', 'front door', 'hop one', 'back door', and 'skip one', all terms used for playing Jump Rope. We kids made 'Tom Walkers'. We felt like we could see the world over when you were on these. They were fun to walk on, especially to jump off a high bank with them.

The daring game was 'Pop the Whip'. Then there were the high banks. We slid down these until they were as slick and as much fun as any slicky slide. Ranking high on the list was the game Hopscotch.

Then there was the Flying Jenny. This was a long pole and in the center of the pole, there was a hole bored in it. When the pole was put on a big stump with a long rod hammered into the stump, one person would get on each end. Someone else would start us off and we would fly. It was kinda dangerous.

These things were literally our way of having fun. We created things to do for fun if we had any spare time from work. There are many children who suffer from boredom or nothing to do. They have time on their hands and it's a nightmare and not a delight. I have never, all through my childhood and as an adult, suffered from having nothing to do. This is because I didn't have things handed to me on a silver platter and was not expecting my parents to be constantly doing things for me for my amusement. That's why children today are bored. They don't know what to do for themselves because things are always done for them. They do not know how to make decisions. When nothing is done for you, you are accustomed to meeting your needs by producing your own ideas.

A game we played inside, Mom made for us, we called Authors. Cards with four identical numbers we called a book. The person to get the most books won. The game consisted of twelve books. We spent many happy hours playing Authors.

SURPRISE

One day Hershel did not go to school. When I came in at noon, he told me, "Come and see the new calf." It was across the road in front of our house. I ran fast and ahead of him and ran into a newly installed barbed wire fence Dad had put up that morning. It went right into my mouth leaving a scar inside my mouth until today. I believe he got a good whipping for that.

BIG SECRET

Then there was the day, Hershel and I were walking home from school. We walked 3 miles each way every day to school. We were 6 years old. There was a very steep hill to the right of where the road ran. The road also had a big drop were there were many rocks that actually built up the road at that point.

I was ahead of him. He said, "Hazel, I would tell you something but I'm afraid it would scare you." He then told me, by my insisting, that the mules were running after us down that hill. Of course, we started running and screaming and dropped books, shoes, lunch pails and all. My Dad was plowing across the creek. He heard us and came waving his hat and yelling. He managed to stop them. Dad went straight to Mr. Wilmer Fowler's and asked him to take the mules out of the pasture. He was renting the pasture from Grandpa Lee.

SWINGING IN THE SWINGSET

If it was possible, we children loved to swing in Mrs. Pearl Taylor's nice rope swing on our way from school. It was such fun to go so very high, high up. I don't see why she allowed this privilege but evidently it didn't bother her. It's a good memory of my childhood.

APRIL FOOL'S DAY

On April Fool's Day, one year when I went to Jamesville School, we decided the day before that we'd play "hooky".

We had picnic lunches, and to the best of my remembrance, we planned to leave when our teacher, Mrs. Effie Fowler, went to the outdoors toilet. Some of the boys raised the big windows and jumped out, some left out the door.

We went to the woods below the school and stayed all evening long. We waded in the creek, picked flowers and ferns, swung from vines, ate our lunches, and had a good time.

THE DAY I MET MY HUSBAND-TO-BE

After we moved to Chireno area, I attended school at Chireno High School. This was a big change for me. It wasn't long before I met Marie Pinkston. Actually, she only lived up the road a couple of miles from me. She was my friend and she told me she had a brother named Cecil. He had already quit school and joined the C.C. Camp.

He was gone during the week, and it was quite a while before I met him. Marie and I visited in each other's home in the daytime on weekends. I don't recall ever spending the night with her or she me.

One Sunday, I went to visit, and Cecil was there. My, I thought he was so good-looking. He was tall and straight shouldered and dressed very well. We visited at their home, then he took out his shoeshine box and shined his shoes. Then he offered to shine and do my shoes. I let him polish them. We were on the front porch of their home, which was located down the lane, back in the woods. This place was on Roy Atkinson's place, I think. It was on the right of the road going toward our house.

Then we all went walking down the road - out to the main road, and all the way to the creek below Roy Atkinson's farm and back. I think we took pictures that day.

Cecil told me many times that he thought I was the most knowledgeable young lady he had ever talked to. I don't remember what we talked about.

I was 15 years of age at this time, of course he was 19 years old.

PARTIES

It was a custom in my teen years for young people to have play parties at their home. If it was summertime, we built fires outside and had them outside. If it was cold, we had them inside.

Just about all the young people walked everywhere. We had some good trails across the woods. We walked from the big house of Mr. Horace Matteauer, down the road in front of our house, then about 3 miles through the woods to the Layton's at Gravel Ridge. Also, we went to other homes. One time I remember going to Verna Moore's house. Also, to Freeman Eblem's, which is the house J.D. Layton lives in today.

We played games, sometimes we had refreshments. We took walks. Some probably were doing more than taking walks.

It was at one of these parties that I got my first tiny kiss from Cecil. I'll never forget it. No, not the kiss but as we were merely engaged, in an innocent "kiss" on the cheek. My dad came out on the porch and yelled bloody murder for me. It scared me and Cecil both almost to death. He just told us to get into the house and stay there.

Later, years after we were married, he told Cecil why. On the ground, in plain sight, there was (evidence) where someone had been making out. Dad apologized for calling us.

COURTSHIP

The parties started our courtship such as it was. Actually, I didn't know him but a year or so before he volunteered for the army.

One night Cecil came to see me, and we went to San Augustine and ate supper at some restaurant. I only remember that I did not eat much at all. I was too nervous. Then that night we went to visit his Uncle William and Aunt Nellie Pinkston there in San Augustine.

Cecil gave me a silver dollar that night that was made in 1921, which was the year he was born. I regret that I guess I spent it.

Cecil and I shared the same birthday, July 19. He was four years older than myself.

Cecil owned a car and he drove it fast. You could hear it coming from afar off. He was a good driver, and contrary to what people thought, he did not drink much then and none after we were married.

POUND SUPPER

We (my family) lived in Mr. Horace's big house with a hall in it on 95 south of Chireno. Mom had told us many times about them having 'pound suppers' when she was a young lady. Everyone who was invited brought a pound of something for food. It was their choice as to what they brought.

She told us we could have a 'pound supper'. We invited friends – we had a lot of people to come. Cecil brought a sack of 'bubble gum' and something else that I've forgotten. We all enjoyed the party.

About this time was when I was very much in love with my future husband, Cecil Pinkston. I was also concerned of his welfare since he had volunteered for U.S. Army, 1942, I believe. I had met him a couple of years prior to this time, but we were getting quite serious by now.

COURTSHIP THROUGH LETTERS

As I mentioned before, Cecil did go into the U. S. Army on June 6th, 1942. Shortly thereafter I began to get letters from him. I was well aware that Cecil had lots of girlfriends, but this didn't bother me much. Especially the ones away from home.

There would be times that I did not hear from him, because of the war, then sometimes there would be four letters at a time. He and I wrote many letters to each other the next two years.

Then he wrote me that he would be home by the time the wind started blowing. I knew he meant March 1st. You see, the mail was censored. I got many letters with words cut out. Sometimes he wrote under a stamp, and it got by.

After Cecil left for service, I was so lonesome. One day we came in from the field – Jesse was about 2 years old – he came running thru the hall and yelling "Hazel, Cecil loves you! You got a letter and he said so!" My! I thought surely Mom has not opened my mail! She had not, this was strictly his words. This was the first letter, but I received many more the next 2 years.

I listened to the war news on the radio and cried and prayed many nights, sometimes about all night long.

WEDDING BELLS RINGING

On March 1st, Cecil drove up at our house. We only shook hands, but it was because there were too many around. I remember it as yesterday. He told me that he was going to Houston and get a job and buy a trailor house for us, and he'd be back after me. He came back in about two weeks, but he still didn't have things quite ready for marriage.

Cecil drove up at Mom's and Dad's on the 23rd day of May. He and I sat in his car and talked, and talked, and talked. Jesse was not quite 4 years of age, but he didn't like about me sitting and talking to Cecil. He got a long stick and kept coming and hitting his car with the stick.

Cecil knew that I didn't want a ring, but he brought me a pretty locket that held 2 pictures. It was in the things that was stolen at Linda's house.

Cecil told me he had the marriage license, and he was going back to Chireno and spend the night with his Uncle Fred Beasley, and he'd be back after me the next morning. We did not have phones or electricity. There was a slight problem. I told Cecil that I would not go until he asked my dad for my hand in marriage. Dad was gone somewhere for the night.

I got up early and got a suitcase packed with such as I had, and then I cooked dinner for him. I had to go borrow sugar for a cake at Leona Dennis' house. She lived in a house that was across the road from where Fee Gartman lives. Cecil was too nervous to eat. You see Dad had not gotten home. I was expecting him any minute, but Cecil was nervous and anxious. So was I.

Finally, Dad got there, but Uncle Hebern (Hebron) was with him, and they were in a hurry to get off fishing. Cecil finally cornered him and 'asked for me'. He told him it would be all right if that's what we wanted and he asked him to "Be good to me, and if he could not do that, he could bring me back."

Dad pulled out his billfold and gave me $25.00 to buy me a new dress. Dad and Mom later, after marriage, gave us 12 hens, a gilt hog, a pretty, white hog. She had some pretty pigs.

Cecil was good to me. He told Dad he would be good to me.

We were on our way shortly. I hated so bad to leave my mom. Elsie went with us. We went on to Nacogdoches and Cecil stopped in front of Beall's Department Store. This store was where the recreation center is now, on the corner near where J.B. White has been for years. Cecil gave me $25.00 also, so Elsie went in with me to buy my wedding dress and trousseau.

I chose a light blue crepe dress. It was a princess type dress and had embroidery all over the front top. I also bought lingerie, two pairs of shoes, I can't remember what else.

We went to Sister Minton's church that night and planned for her to marry us, but she did not have license to do so. We went across the street and woke up another lady minister – Sister Rosella Owens. She married us. Elsie was our only attendant.

WEDDING NIGHT

Cecil and I went back to his mom's home to spend the night. Mr. Pinkston was away working and there was no one there except her and the children.

It rained all night and her house leaked. It seemed like she had to check on the leaks quite often. Cecil finally told her to never mind the leaking and stay out of our room.

I had planned to go back to Mom's the next day for our wedding dinner, but Cecil did not want to go. This bothered me because I knew that she would be expecting us, and she was.

Also, I did not have a wedding shower. He said, "We don't need one." I was to learn this was his proud ways. He had the trailor. It was small. He had everything, dishes, pots & pans, and linens. Also, he had the cabinets stocked with all kinds of spices and supplies.

The first place we lived at was Galena Park, near Houston.

EARLY DAYS OF OUR MARRIAGE

Cecil was a very independent person. He was really good about taking me back to Mom and Dad's. I had not taken my personal things with me when I married, so we made many trips to visit, and I'd always have a box or two to take to our house.

Especially I remember getting my photographs. When I got home, I found the picture of Cecil and I almost ruined. It was a 5x7. Jesse had taken this picture and a lead pencil and scribbled all over our faces. Remember, he wasn't yet 4 years old, but he was very angry because Cecil came and got me. Incidentally, after Jesse was grown, he thought lots of Cecil and vice versa.

Mom would give us eggs and milk or whatever she had on hand. This took some time for Cecil to get used to. He never, ever wanted a handout.

PLACES WE LIVED AFTER MARRIAGE

I mentioned before that Cecil owned a small factory built trailor or mobile home, on the model of an air stream trailor. We lived at Galena Park a few months, then went to Beaumont and lived awhile there.

In the fall of the year, we came back to East Texas. Cecil parked the trailor where Uncle Hebern (Hebron) lived, off the road between where the Gartman's and Floyd Gartman lives now. He trapped some, I believe.

He pulled this trailor and parked it at a couple more places around the community nearby. Then sold the trailor.

Then before the weather got bad, Cecil rented the house in front of Fee Gartman. (No house there now, it burned long ago.) He farmed that year, and we had a pretty garden. Charles was born here the next April 28, 1945.

It was here we lived, Cecil would often times get me to drive the car up and down the road. He'd sit on the hood of the car with his gun and shoot rabbits. Sometimes he'd kill several. It's a miracle I didn't kill him, me not knowing how to drive.

We bought our first property the fall of 1945. Cecil drove his car too fast for me when we first married. He heard of this little farmhouse with about 12 acres of land for sale. He asked me "Would you rather have the car or the place?" We decided to sell the car and buy our first place.

So, we moved to our first home that he had bought. It cost $500.00. I believe there was 12 acres, a house that was livable, no fireplace. We had a 55-gallon barrel for a heater. Also, we had a pretty good barn and lot which was fenced. Dad had given me some chickens and a pretty, white sow, which found pigs while we lived there. I think all the pigs died because of a severe cold spell. They froze to death. I hated this place, so Cecil sold it for $1000.00 cash. Charles spent his first Christmas here.

When Charles was about 8 months old, we went to Orange for a while. Cecil worked there. We lived in a small rented trailor house, real near a store. I'd go out there every day and get us a coke. Charles would drink a whole small coke then, one every day.

Next, he bought some land, just a lot down the lane from where Pinky Ma and Pinky Pa lived off Looneville Rd. Cecil built this little house, which was a three-room house. It was neat and nice, but he had a chance to sell it, so he did. He made money on it. It was with the profit of this that Cecil bought his first used truck in 1946.

We moved back to Dad's farm in the upper house. It was here that we lived when Charles started walking. Also, Clifford Pinkston lost his life by a car hitting him. He was full of the Holy Ghost. This was in 1946.

I think Cecil raised some truck patches while we lived here.

Then we moved to the 'red house'. Dad wanted to put some renters in the upper house, and it would be closer for me to be near Mom. It was here that Mary was born. This was 1946.

We moved from here to Chireno and lived upstairs in Grandpa Lee's house. I remember making Mary little print dresses while we lived here. She was 3 months old. It was while we lived here that Cecil bought his first brand new G.M.C. truck – 1947.

Cecil went to West Texas to work with the truck and left me with Mom and Dad. They had moved in Mrs. Nena Posey's house near Chireno. I very well remember crying a lot because I missed him so bad. He was not gone long until he came back. He bought a trailor chaise and built a trailor house on it. He built this right on the roadside, in front of the Nena Posey house. We lived in the trailor house there awhile.

Quite soon, Cecil moved this trailor back down to the farm and parked it alongside the road next to the garden. It was near Mom and Dad's house. Cecil was fishing at that time commercially.

Then in April of 1948, he moved the trailor to Nacogdoches and parked it near Pinky Ma and Pinky Pa's house. This was down the lane near the house we had bought. This is where we lived when Linda was born.

Perhaps we moved into our house in June or July of 1948. Cecil had done a lot of clearing the land and I had fixed the house some.

This house burned in March of 1951. We had been to West Texas the fall before and we had had a grass fire and burned a little shed outside, so the insurance company had canceled our home insurance. I had gotten a letter with a refund and hadn't gone and taken out more insurance, therefore we had no insurance. This was a tragic loss for us. We owed one payment on a new refrigerator and that was all we owed on anything.

We had made a 20x20 big room on the front of the house and a small room on the left side which we used for a sleeping porch in the summer. On the right-hand side, Cecil had made a shed room for a bedroom. We had the house furnished with good furniture. Plenty of good beds. Mrs. Pinkston had given me her cedar chifforobe. Cecil had bought me a new pedal sewing machine that cost $139.00. The fall before I had bought all the children plus myself new winter coats.

The things that we missed the most were our pictures. Edward was small and everywhere we went; he would get out and say, "Our house burned up and burned all our pictures." This was the way I felt about all the quilts I had made. Saying nothing of all the nice little dresses I had made for my little girls.

I remember Hershel coming to see us and when he walked thru the house and saw how completely it was destroyed, he said to me "I wish this would have been my house, because I didn't have much to lose."

Cecil and Dad had gone to Jasper to sell some fishing equipment that Cecil wanted to sell. Mom was with me, and we were at Sister Minton's church that night. It only seems like yesterday, that Pinky Pa came running to the church during the service and said, "Cecil and Hazel's house has burned." I was relieved when he said that. I thought he was going to tell me that Cecil and Dad had a wreck and got killed.

Cecil was so devastated. He did not want help from anyone. The D.A.V. brought him a check for $50.00, also some blankets, etc. The family all gave us a little money and we started over.

We used some of the framing for another little house, borrowed money to build another one, near Pinky Ma. This was in order to build first and clean up the burned house later. We did this by ourselves and moved into the house in 2 months. We only made a three-room house at that time. Later we made 2 more rooms plus a shed room at the back. This was the only place we actually lived except to go off to West Texas to work in the fall.

Also, Cecil rented a house near Chireno one time and fished there a few months. Another time he rented a house down near Alazan and fished. We were only camping like then, as we still maintained our home at Nacogdoches on Looneville Rd.

After Cecil's death, we could not stay at the house, so I rented a house down the street from the Minton's church. We lived here until the last of May 1965 and Charles and LaNelle married. Mary, Linda, Edward, and I moved to Mississippi. This was a very, very hard thing for me to do. The girls wanted to go; I did not go with the intention of staying but I did almost 10 years.

We moved into the parsonage on the back of the church and lived there for a few months. Then I bought a used trailor and put it down on the creek bank near Granny Russell, near Sister Jean's. Jesse moved down there.

Later I moved the trailor on the left side of the road near the church on the highway 49. I lived here when Mary and Bobby married.

Then I moved the same trailor up the road a few miles on the left down in a flat place. Another move was over on the hill, and I do mean hill. I was following Sister Jean around. I told the kids that I wasn't doing this anymore. I would buy a lot myself and park the trailor permanently. I lived here when Edward and Debbie married.

In 1971 I bought a new mobile home and bought a lot behind the church. I lived here until I moved back to Texas.

Charles moved my trailor back to Texas in 1974 down on the farm and parked it at the 'little red house'. Laverne and Aubry owned the farm by then. I lived at this place and until after Dad and Hershel died, then Mom and I moved to the present place on Durst St. at Pine Lake Estates. This being a HUD Section 8 housing project. We moved here in 1982.

OUR VISIT TO GRANDPA LEE

We had not been married very long and we went to visit Grandpa Lee and Mrs. Myrtie. It was cool weather. They asked us to spend the night. Looking back, I can't imagine that Cecil wanted to stay, but we did.

I remember this so well, Mrs. Myrtie said "Hazel, you can sleep with me in the fireplace room where it's warm, and Cecil can sleep with Pop in the back room where it's so cold." So, we did. In the night, sometime Cecil forgot that he wasn't in bed with me, he was half-asleep, he got a bit amorous and started poking Grandpa. I'm sure he thought no one would ever know about it, but the next morning when Grandpa got up, he was putting on his shoes by the fireplace. He started laughing. Then he only said "Cecil, you forgot who you were sleeping with, didn't you?" Cecil told me about it, after we left. This is the first time I've told this funny.

FAST DRIVING

When we were first married, Cecil did drive too fast to suit me. However, he was a very good driver.

One time, he and I were coming in from Beaumont. He was pulling the trailor house with his car. This trailor was probably about 40' long. It was not an Air Stream but was made like one and resembled one a lot.

We were coming from San Augustine direction and at the bridge on Hi-way 21, just before we got to the cut-off that went to Chireno, another truck came out from the cut-off, and we were meeting head on. Cecil blinked the lights, but he could not stop, and the other fellow did not stop.

The Lord was with us and believe me, I was calling on Him! Cecil had to ride the rail to let us both pass on that narrow bridge. It's a wider bridge there now.

Another time we were blessed to not have a wreck was in the year of 1949. Cecil went out in West Texas to move some people named Perkins. Mr. and Mrs. Perkins, Cecil, and I, and I believe Charles went with us.

It was a long trip there and they loaded the furniture and everything. It was a turnaround trip. I believe this was somewhere near Big Springs. Anyway, it was in the night. We were trucking along, and a truck came in on a bridge with us and Cecil actually jumped on the walkway of the bridge and broke the 4x8 runners on his truck off. He also damaged the bridge. This wasn't just a short bridge but rather a long bridge over deep water. It was deep, deep down under.

I had gotten Elsie to keep the girls for me. She told me when I left "If anything happens, I'm keeping these kids." It almost did.

Cecil did have one wreck several years later and on a bridge. It hurt him and some other people also, not serious.

The last job Cecil worked at was at Dewitt's Hatchery. He did numerous different jobs there, working at night. Mr. Bob Dewitt was a friend to Cecil and also a Mr. Richard (Dick) Campbell. Even after Cecil was hospitalized for several months, they let him go back to work. He was not a truck driver from Dewitt's, as the article in the paper concerning his death stated.

MY DAY IN THE WOODS

One day I was fishing in the river bottom, near the Attoyac River on Highway 21. I had been hand poling all day and had an enjoyable time. This was about the year 1960. I had not been afraid, although I had thought what if something happened to me down here in these woods and no one knew where I was.

Pinky Ma and Pinky Pa were temporarily living there at a house right before reaching the river. Pinky Pa was fishing and hunting. I had just gotten to their house when an insane man came out from the same place I had been. His clothing was almost torn off him and he was scratched badly. Also, he was hungry. Mr. Pinkston gave him food. He knew the man, but he was in bad shape. The Lord watches over his own.

114

OUR HOME BURNING

When our house burned, we were at church. Pinky Pa came to the church to tell us about it. This was in the year 1951. I had bought all the children and myself a new winter coat that fall. When I drove up to our house, cars were as far as you could see on both sides of the road, sightseeing.

This was Charles' first year in school. Cecil had bought him new overalls and some blue and red handkerchiefs, little boy size. As we stopped, Charles said, "All my handkerchiefs burned up."

Edward was more concerned about all our photographs burning up. He was only two years old but everywhere we went, he'd get out and say, "All our pictures burned up." All the time, I was thinking about my boxes of love letters and all my new quilts I had just made. So, you see, it's not just the big things we miss most.

GOD WILL PROVIDE

When our house burned in 1951, we lost everything. I had given Elsie an old timey ice box, that you put blocks of ice in. We had bought us a big, nice refrigerator. I got it at Western Auto. After my house burned, she bought herself a new refrigerator and the place where she purchased hers gave her the old timey box back to give to me. I was thankful for one at all.

EARLY DAYS OF DRIVING

I did not drive for many years because I was afraid to drive. After my children started to school, and there was no school bus by our home because we were in the city limits, I had to learn to drive. Anyway, Cecil bought me a new 1953 Ford which cost $3500.00.

We were in West Texas and Cecil wanted me to bring him his lunch. I had taken him to work. Elsie went with me. On the way back, she wanted me to stop at a house on the opposite side of the road to buy some buttermilk. I kept telling her I couldn't drive up that narrow road. There was a culvert there also and she said, "Yes, you can."

When we got back along there to turn off, I wheeled in that drive, kind of like a teenager. I had not even seen this man squatted down by his mailbox. He started trying to move and fell backwards. It scared him worse than it did me. Thank God, I didn't kill him.

DAD COMES TO VISIT ME

One day, Dad drove up, which wasn't unusual, but he told me, "Get ready, I've come to take you to get your driver's license." I tried to beg off. I'd been driving for several years but had never taken the time to go and get my driver's license. I told Dad, "I can't go today. My car is in the shop." Then he said, "I have a brand-new pickup out there. You can use it." I knew I needed to go, so I decided I'd go ahead and take my written test that day. Then I'd have my car the next day to take the driver's test. I did just that and passed everything with flying colors.

LABOR CAMP LOCKNEY, TEXAS

Just about every fall, Cecil and I and the children went to West Texas. He would carry a crew to work for him and he worked also. The last two years, he did not haul cotton, he worked at the gin. We lived in what we called the labor camp in Lockney, Texas. The cabin was one big, square room. The bathrooms and bathhouse were in the center of the camp. We had to carry our water inside to cook with. These places were very warm. We had been to West Texas that fall before Edward was due. We went back home, and Edward was born on a Saturday, December 30, 1949.

OUR TRIP TO ORANGE, TEXAS WITH JESSE DRIVING

One day Cecil called and me and asked me to get my brother, Jesse, to drive me and the children to Orange. Cecil had a big, long, trailor truck, but he needed his other truck. Jesse was thirteen years old, but he'd been driving for some time. We started on our trip. The children always liked to ride in the back of the truck. Usually, Edward would ride in the front with me.

I always put quilts, pillows, lawn chairs, ice cooler, etc., in the back for their comfort and pleasure. We were about twelve miles from Jasper when the truck caught fire under the hood, filling the cab full of smoke all of a sudden. Jesse pulled off the road, jumped out, raised the hood, and got the fire put out. Several people stopped to assist us. I'm sure they were concerned, seeing a woman with all those kids and the truck smoking as it was.

The children took everything out of the back of the truck and put them under the beautiful trees. It was an ideal place to have truck trouble. These men tried and tried to get the truck to crank. The wires were burned really terrible. One gentleman told me that he was going into Jasper and Jesse could ride with him and get a wrecker to come and pull us in. I gave Jesse a check and he went. I was concerned that he may not get anyone to come and him being a kid.

We waited for one and half or two hours and he hadn't come. I had prayed all that time. I didn't feel really safe, even then, out there and it was getting close to dark. I told the children, "Let's load up." They said, "Mama, what are we going to do?" I told them, "We are going to go." You see, I did not know how to drive. Charles was about eight years of age. He was very anxious to help me. He said, "Mama, I'll shift the gears for you if you get it cranked." We all got in the cab of the truck. I turned the key in that switch and started praying, "In Jesus Name, In Jesus Name, let this truck crank!" and He did just that!

Charles did shift the gears and we headed toward Jasper. We met Jesse and the wrecker several miles down the road. I'll never forget how big his eyes were when he saw me driving. The wrecker man would not take any money. Jesse drove the truck on to Orange. Dad and Cecil raised that hood and could not believe that I had gotten it to crank, and we had gone on that far in the truck and it burned so badly.

We can get an answer for many things calling on His name, which is Jesus. I have drawn strength many times from this very incident. There is power in prayer!

CECIL ON THE RIVER WHEN A STORM ARRIVED

Once we were at Mom's and Dad's and Cecil had gone to the river to either put out trot lines or perhaps run his lines. I'm sure I drove him down there, but the children and I were at Mom's. It came a very bad storm, at least we all thought so. Bad lightning, thunder, and wind. I went to the river once to see if I could hear his outboard motor. I knew Cecil could not hear the thunder rolling especially with his outboard motor running. We thought surely by the time he felt the wind so fierce; he'd be on.

I was so concerned and praying every breath. Finally, someone saw him coming around the curve in the road. They said, "He's been hurt. His face has blood all over it." We all went to meet him. He had on a red leather cap and all the soaking rain he'd been in had made his cap fade and run the red color all over his face. He wasn't aware of how he looked. I don't recall that he was frightened of the storm.

LIVING AT MR. AND MRS. REESE'S ON BEAUMONT & ORANGE HIGHWAY

Cecil was acquainted with everyone who had little stores on the highways. These people told him they had an extra room that they would rent to us for the summer. This was a good location dividing equally the distances between two large towns. This room had no bathroom. We used a potty and took baths in a washtub. This was different for the children even though I'd known it was not uncommon.

Cecil made good that year, making many trips to East Texas, Houston, etc. Dad was raising produce on the farm and Cecil sold much of that. One particular time, though, Dad had brought several sacks of green peas that he had not sold. Cecil sold some but we had several sacks left. Dad told me to shell them if we didn't sell them. So, I did. Mrs. Reese was a very sweet and accommodating person. She told me to put the peas in the commercial freezer. She also said she knew some people who put their peas in the freezer without washing them. I did them this way and they were fine. I would not recommend doing this if you plan to keep the peas in the freezer for very long.

I told you at the beginning that we used a wash tub to bathe the children in. The tub had a bad place on the rim of it. I guess it was broken. The children were aware of the fact. One day, Charles was bathing. He had made himself lots of soap bubbles and started going round and round in the tub. He cut his backend quite badly. I'm sure he carries the scar to this day.

GOING TO ORANGE

The next summer after Cecil bought the new car for me, he called me one night to come to Orange and bring him something. Seemed to have been a truck part. I told him I didn't feel safe to drive that far, since I had not been driving very long. He assured me that I could. On the way down, I had a water hose to break. I was near a store, but they could not fix it, no water hose. The man told me to drive slowly and go back down the road I'd just traveled. They could put one on for me. I was very concerned about my car, but it did not hurt it. I made the trip there and back to Nacogdoches with no more problems.

LEAVING LINDA & MARY AT FAYE & LAVERNE'S

Many times, the girls would not want to go along with us. LaVerne and Aubry and Faye and Dean were so very good to keep them for me many times. I already mentioned someplace that Elsie did also. The only thing, she wasn't living in East Texas very much of the time when they were small.

Many a time, we would be packed and ready to go the very day school was out. The children's teachers were so kind to just mail their report cards and records to them. We always had a post office box at the post office. Lest we forget, it was P.O. Box 211. Our home address on Looneville Road was 1516.

We left home the following morning about 2:00 or 3:00 A.M. We had to get to the farmer's market at Houston early. Cecil bought trailor loads of melons and then he had a bob truck that he unloaded onto, selling at the stores. Many times, he would sell a whole load and return for another load.

Perhaps I've mentioned this in another paragraph somewhere, but I can still see the motel which was near Orange on the Beaumont Highway that we rented for several weeks at a time and for consecutive years also. One night, Cecil was so anxious to be ready, he put our packed suitcases we had in the back of the truck the night before. We had two. We assumed someone took the one that had his clothing and mine in it. This was a time when the girls were going to stay with Faye and Dean. I believe we came all the way back to

Nacogdoches. We had gotten to Lufkin looking for the suitcase, also to get more clothing.

RENTED A PLACE DOWN HIGHWAY 7

Cecil loved to fish. He was not trucking now, so we rented this farmhouse near the Angelina River from a very nice man, his name might have been Mr. Poskey. It was near the river, and he was fishing in a new area. Never did he catch as many on the Angelina River as he did the Attoyac River. One day, Dad and Mom came down there to go fishing in the creek, which was in the closed pasture in front of our house. We had been down there several times fishing. There were lots of snakes down there. We had permission to go into the field with the cows.

As we were coming out, Mom and I were ahead. Dad and Linda were still fishing. All at once, this long, long horned brindle cow started making a funny noise and pawing on the ground. Mom said, "Don't run. The cow is trying to get the herd to stampede." She did just that. Mom had on a big hat and stood her ground with that cow by waving her hat and hollering at the cow. We got on to the house, so thankful they didn't get us.

In a half hour or so, Dad and Linda came in, so excited and said that cow had done them the same way. Dad used his fishing pole to bluff her. He said he'd already told Linda to hit the creek. God was good to us, and we never went back in that pasture again.

ELSIE AND I GET A SCARE

One night Elsie came up to see me for a while and all my children were gone. Cecil was in bed. I thought he was asleep. He was not well at the time. Elsie had Melvin with her, and she had left him in the car asleep.

As we were sitting at the table enjoying ourselves, we were working on a quilt pattern called The Drunkard Path. I heard the living room doorknob turn and it sounded like someone was trying to break in. I went to check, looking out the glass window, and saw a woman there. Sure enough, as I started to open the door, she was pushing to get in, but I pushed harder and got the door bolted. I remember I said, "No, you don't need in here."

I went back and told Elsie, "I'll have to call Cecil, but I sure hate to excite him." I knew he would get his gun. I went into the bedroom and told him the circumstances. He got his gun, and I went out with him. About the same time, two police cars drove up. I spied the woman. She had squatted down under a big air cooler which was in our bedroom window. She was one more intoxicated woman. The patrol apprehended her without any resistance. I did not know the woman. Jesus was watching over us on that dark night.

CECIL'S PARENTS

PINKY MA AND PINKY PA PINKSTON

Lester (Pinky Pa) Pinkston was born on October 14, 1894. He was married to Mary Lee (Pinky Ma) Beasley Pinkston who was born on April 17, 1894. Pinky Pa served as a private in the U.S. Army in World War I. He passed on November 10, 1971 at 77 years of age. Pinky Ma passed on October 28, 1981 at 87 years of age. They are both buried at the Upper Chireno Cemetery in Nacogdoches County. They had seven children, of which my husband, Cecil was the oldest.

PINKY PA'S STORIES TO CHILDREN

One day, a man rode up on a horse bringing news to another man that a horse had thrown his brother and killed him. The man used chewing tobacco and he spit on the ground. He said, "Well, it could have been worse." The gentleman bringing the sad news said, "What do you mean? He's dead as hell." This man spit again and said, "It could have been me." Pinky Pa said this was true. He knew the people.

PINKY PA AS A GUARD

Pinky Pa got himself a job as a guard. He needed this job badly. It seemed that the man who hired him was going to try him out for his ability to obey orders and his ability to handle this kind of job. Pinky Pa wanted very much to be impressive and keep his job. He accomplished his desires. Quite soon after he started, he knocked down a great big man who wanted to come up without the proper identification papers. I assume he kept his job.

PINKY PA'S FAVORITE

This may not have been true, I'm not sure. Why did he buy Charles a new suit? A three-piece suit? Why did he buy him nice big toys? Why did he buy him his first vehicle, a Jeep? I suppose I was wrong to think this, but I had three more children who noticed.

I know Pinky Pa really loved Edward. They spent many hours talking on that little front porch. I could hardly ever get up early enough in the summer months to have Edward for breakfast. He had already eaten with his Pinky Pa.

OUR CHILDREN

CHARLES

It was Saturday, April 28, 1945, that I was to become a mother for the very first time. I had not had any bad problems with my pregnancy with Charles.

I ate all the popcorn I wanted. You see, this was what I craved. You could not always find it in the store, so someone told Cecil about a man who raised popcorn in his fields. Cecil went to see him. He gave Cecil a big field sack full of popcorn. This was on the cob, but I didn't mind. I popped it in a skillet with lots of grease and got fat as a hog.

I had picked berries a big part of the day that I went into labor. In the field where we lived there was a bumper crop of dew berries. I would carry me a bucket or something to sit on and I could pick a gallon without moving. The best of my recollections, I had picked a washtub full that day.

I think I recall the first pain, which started in my back. This was while I was washing the berries. I don't remember if I got my berries canned or not, but I believe I did.

There was a lot of the relatives visiting at Mom and Dad's that day and night to go fishing. We lived in a house across the road from where Fee Gartman lives now. The house is no longer there.

Cecil went after Dr. Taylor Mast, who lived at Chireno. He didn't get in any hurry to come. He might have come and gone back home for a while; I don't know.

Cecil and Hershel were both my "pullers". They each held my hand when the pains would come, and I pulled on them.

I believe Grandma Hooper was there too. I had an awful time with my labor with Charles. He was such a big baby. I thought it was terrible.

Finally, he made his appearance at 11:30 pm, weighing 11 lbs. and a little over. Cecil had me believing I was going to have a girl, so I was surprised when I had a big boy. I remember Grandpa Lee coming to see me and my baby. He told me "Hazel, you can lay there and look at that baby and worry yourself to death, watching him jump, make all the facial motions and all of the things little babies do. Those things are only natural."

I had made a lot of little gowns for the new baby. He could not wear them at all.

Charles was a good baby. He did get his days and nights mixed up for a while, but nothing unusual. He was a delight. He grew and grew. When he was six months old, we were living at Orange for a while and lived near a little store. I'd go to the store with him and buy him a coke. He'd drink a whole bottle. They came in the 10 oz. bottles then.

Charles started walking at age 1 year. He was, as a baby, fast on foot. He would run from me. When he was small, it was a game with us. Later, after he was a good size little boy, he would run from me. One day, I caught him. I think that kinda changed his mind about running.

MARY

It was on a Sunday night that my labor began with Mary. Since I had already been thru one labor, I knew what to expect.

I had the pains all night and would doze off to sleep occasionally and awaken with the reminder that I was about to be a mama again.

I waited until it was daylight before I told Cecil to go get the doctor. I wanted the school bus to come and go before I sent after Mom.

We lived in the 'little red house' or the 'playhouse' as it's known now. When Cecil went for Dr. Taylor Mast, who lived at Chireno, he was out on another sick call. I believe Cecil made three trips up there.

Mary did not wait for the doctor to come. She came into this world, with just Mom and me present. I was very scared. Mom assured me she was alright, and she was. The doctor finally came, and I was glad.

Elsie was pregnant with Nathan, so she stayed out in the yard until after Mary came.

Mary was born on Monday, October 14, 1946, at 9:50 am. She weighed 9 lbs., 8 oz.

Mary was a fretful baby for some time after she was born. I recall sitting in front of the fireplace and rocking her. I was also introduced to afterbirth pains, which I had not had with the first baby. This I was to learn, is the way everyone does, that is, does not have after birth pains with the first child. These were almost as bad as labor pains.

Mary was a beautiful baby. Her hair was dark and curly. I remember her having a little pink crochet dress and I'd put her a cap on and dress her up. She was so sweet. Mary cried a lot. I think she had colic. I could not hold her all the time since I had another baby. Then on wash days, it was tough. I'm speaking of Charles.

LINDA

We had moved to Nacogdoches by this time. We had already bought the house on Looneville Road, but I wanted to clean and get the house fixed up before we moved in.

We were living in a trailor house that Cecil had made himself. It was one long trailor, but I had partitioned it off: kitchen, bedroom and living room. I had papered the trailor. This was the first of my wallpapering but wasn't to be the last. I remember well that it was a little flowered print. I didn't know it had to be matched, but the print was so small, it didn't look bad. We had this trailor parked out back of Mr. and Mrs. Pinkston down the lane from our house we just bought.

Back to the baby who was about to be born. The night before, we had all walked to Sister Minton's to church. There was a trail thru the woods, and it was nearer to go that way. Pinky Ma, Tincey, Big Girl, Charles, Mary, and I went to church. They helped me with Charles and Mary.

After I got home, my back started hurting me very bad. I knew I was in labor; it was time to go to the clinic. This clinic was located on East Main, perhaps it was the building where there's an insurance company now.

It must have been two o'clock in the morning when we went. My doctor, whom I'd already been going to, examined me, and told me I was not in labor, to go home. I walked back out to the front desk where Cecil was waiting and told him "Pay this man. I'm not coming back here." He paid him. We went back home.

The next morning, I told him, "I am not going back to that doctor, so go and see if you can find someone else to take me."

This was the day I met Dr. James G. Taylor. His office at that time was over Commercial Bank. Cecil had gone up there and talked to him. He told him to bring me up there. I was in the last stage of labor by then. When he looked at me outside his desk, he didn't even take me back to his office. He said, "Take her on to the hospital. I can tell by looking at her face, the baby is ready."

I remember how long those stairs were going up and back down. I don't remember exactly how long it was after I got to the hospital before her birth, but not long.

Here, I soon found out that I had another little girl. She was born Thursday, May 13, 1948. She weighed 8 lbs., 9 oz. No one could doubt she was a Pinkston.

I had a white bassinet at this time for her. Linda was the best baby I had. She was easily pleased as a baby. All she wanted was to be fed and kept dry. It almost worried me because she was so good. I was to find out later that her disposition was, that she didn't want anyone to bother her. When she was sick, she didn't want me to pay attention to her but rather leave her alone.

EDWARD

We lived at the house on Looneville Road when Edward was born.

We had been to West Texas that fall, and I had done a little field work. I mostly 'weighed cotton' and kept books for all the hands that Cecil was working. We had been home about one month.

I had wanted so bad for my last baby to be born before Christmas. I was so big and miserable. I didn't want to go to Mom and Dad's for our Christmas and me pregnant again. He did not choose to come early.

By this time, my labor pains were not nearly as long as in previous times. I began to have the pains up in the day, and it seems as if I didn't have anyone to keep my other children. Finally, I got them, probably to Pinky Ma, and Cecil took me to the hospital. Buddy's wife, Hazel, went with me.

By the time I got to the hospital, I was about ready to have my baby, but they didn't believe me. The problem was, they could not get up with Dr. James G. Taylor. I got so mad because they wouldn't take me to the delivery room. I finally told the nurse, "I should have stayed home and had the baby." Then they literally ran down the hall with me, telling me "Don't breathe, hold back." and all that clamor. They barely got me on the table when he came. I learned later that Dr. T.J. Pennington actually delivered him.

Edward was born on Saturday, December 30, 1949, at 6:47 pm. He weighed 8 lbs., 6 oz. I don't remember if anyone spent the night that night with me or not. The next night was New Year's Eve and I recollect how excited I got when all the sirens started blowing. Laverne was spending that night with me.

I had planned to have a tubal while I was in the hospital with my baby. Dr. Taylor said he would not do it then because I needed some other work done and he wanted to wait 6 weeks. I was brought home from the hospital in an ambulance. Mary said she associated the ambulance with a hearse. I remember the day I went home. It had started raining and freezing. Everything got really white. Laverne was with me a few days to help me.

My, how tickled Charles, Mary, and Linda were to have a little baby brother. They wanted to get on the bed with me, so they could see him good. Edward was a very good baby when he was little. I recall him sleeping all night without wetting his diaper when he was about 6 months old. Charles and Mary were big enough by then to help me quite a bit. They could run errands, getting diapers, soap, pins and especially swinging and talking to him.

I must say this, when he was 6 or 8 months old, I had gotten a wringer washer and I had it on the back porch. There was a 'little hole' beside the porch that the kids played in. When it rained, it was a puddle. As I washed, I let him play in that mud hole, he sure enjoyed it. It was sand and wasn't bad. Edward sure did like to keep clean, by the time he was 2 years old or so, he would take several baths per day and change clothes.

HONORABLE MENTIONS

When Mary was three months old, she fell off the bed. I was at Elsie's. They lived down Easy Street at Chireno. We were outside and heard her crying. We ran inside and couldn't find her. She had fallen off at the backside of the bed.

When Charles was about ten months old, he put all his cans of milk through a small hole in the back room. One day he was looking down through the hole and got stuck. About half his body was through the hole. Elsie got him out.

When Mary was about twelve years old, I was sewing for the girls, and they were cooking dinner. She had turned the gas on and thought the stove lit, but it didn't. She struck another match, and it singed her hair. She didn't know what had happened. She began saying, "There's a cat in the oven." She didn't realize it was her hair.

EDWARD GIVES MORAL SUPPORT

After all the other children were away from home, many was the time when I'd think I could not manage financially or otherwise. Edward would tell me, "Mama, don't worry about these things. You know you'll figure them out. You always have."

EDWARD PROTECTING MARY AND LINDA

One night, Cecil and I were both working on a public job. Charles was gone. Edward told the girls that he'd protect them, not to worry. They were ironing. He got a big, long butcher knife and lay down on a pallet near them and went to sleep. When I got in, they were laughing about his protection. He meant well.

WHEN WE RENTED A HOUSE IN CHIRENO

One year we moved to Chireno. Cecil was net fishing, unable to work. This was on the road going toward Gloryland. The kids thought this was fun. We had an outdoor toilet, well in the back yard, and a fireplace for heat. They enjoyed all of this because they had never lived without conveniences of that sort.

One afternoon, they were all out in the back yard, drawing water out of the well. You see, we came home, and the kitty was missing. The kitty was in the well, dead. Their dad told them they'd have to draw all the water out of the well, so that's what they proceeded to do. They started daring each other to throw a bucket of that cold well water on that Daddy while he was washing the car. I think it was Charles who threw the cold water on him, and I think he ran, ran, and ran.

HAPPY LINDA

Mrs. Cole, the third-grade teacher, asked her class to write a paper on what they'd like to be if they could be something or somebody else. Linda didn't write anything. She said she was happy to be herself, when questioned by her teacher. Mrs. Cole told me that the children wrote all kinds of animals and people's names. She was impressed with Linda.

QUITE POSITIVE

When Linda was in the second grade at school, she told her teacher, Mrs. Fain, that Mama planted some berry cuttings the day before. Mrs. Fain asked her if they were Boysen berries. She looked her straight in the eye and said, "I'm sure they were not poison or Mom would not have planted them."

BOYS WILL BE BOYS

Once we were over at Pinky Ma and Pinky Pa's house on Westview. The kids liked to play outside. Buddy and Hazel's children were over there also. Their boys and mine decided to put some of Mrs. Copeland's hens under a tub. I think it killed the chickens. I've forgotten for sure.

EDWARD SWIMMING

Once we had a Fourth of July outing at the Cottingham Bridge on the River near Dad's farm. We had already had lunch and ice cream. Some of the grown kids had gone swimming in the river but someone mentioned going over a little farther to the slough and letting the younger ones go in swimming.

The children all ran ahead, and several had already gotten in the water. Some small child had jumped in. I was always behind, but I saw Dad jump in shoes, clothes and all and I said, "It's probably Edward" and it was.

We had been living at Orange and I'd take the kids walking around swimming pools and Edward had seen them dive in. I guess he thought that was the way to swim. No bad results, but it could have been.

EDWARD AND LINDA SELLING CHINQUAPINS

We had a Chinquapin tree over our bathroom window. There were a few other trees around also. Edward and Linda would pick them up and go sell them at Mr. Prudhome's store for 50 cents a gallon.

LINDA AT LOCKNEY SCHOOL

After the children were in school, we'd go on our pilgrimage to West Texas early, so the children could start to school. There were many Spanish children in the schools at Lockney even then. The children walked to school if it wasn't too bad. One day at noon, they came in for lunch and Linda announced she wasn't going back to school. I told her, "Yes, you definitely are going back. I'll go see what the problem is." She told me, "They won't give me a book and I'm having to sit on the floor." That did sound like a pretty good reason to not relish going back to school. At any rate, I went back with her and talked to her teacher. Things improved somewhat.

WHEN CHARLES WAS SMALL, 6 MONTHS PERHAPS

Cecil and James were going to town for some purpose, and they wanted to take Charles with them. I was very reluctant to let him go, but James said, "I'll hold him in my lap." We didn't have car seats or seat belts in the year of 1944.

This little errand was not to take very long, but it did. Cecil had to come to a sudden stop. James was not holding Charles good. Charles hit the windshield in the car and cut his forehead quite badly. They had taken him to the hospital and had stitches put in. Needless to say, I was already in a state of panic before they arrived. You know the Bible says, "Be angry and sin not." I'm quite sure that I did sin that day because I was mad! I felt it was carelessness on both Cecil and James' part. I think they got the message, too.

CHARLES GOES TO TOWN WITH DAD

Cecil was going into town; I believe to get something at the Palace Seed Store. I know that's where he parked. Charles was two or three years of age and wanted to go with his daddy. Cecil left him in the car, I'm sure giving him orders to stay put. But Charles never stayed put long at that age. He still doesn't!

Charles decided he'd get out and walk around a little. But what do you know? The car got lost. He started crying and was frightened. A policeman came along and found the child, talked to him, trying to find out where he lived. He told them his name and that he lived up a big hill. You did go up a hill to reach our home, but then the area was very level where the homes were located.

Cecil was frightened when he got to the car. He went to the police station and there he was. They had calmed Charles down and were entertaining him. All was well.

LINDA CUTS HER FINGER

I do not remember how Linda had gotten her finger cut, but it was sore and hurting badly. We were on our way to Orange with a load of watermelons, leaving home late in the evening. Linda did not usually cry but she did that night. She was about two and a half or three years of age. I can remember it as yesterday. How could you forget when she must have said, "I want a Band-Aid." "I need a Band-Aid." a hundred or more times, over and over, she uttered those words. There were no stores open. She stood up beside her dad or under his arm.

Then all at once, just below Kirbyville, Cecil saw a whole herd of cattle bedded down in the middle of the two-lane road. I'll never know how he missed hitting any of the cows. He went between one, then another and did not hit any of them. The angels of the Lord were encamped above us that night, protecting the whole family. God is so good to his people.

CHARLES SOLD PEANUTS

When we lived in the labor camp at Lockney, Texas in 1950, Charles received his first taste of salesmanship. I bought raw peanuts and parched them. We bagged the peanuts into small bags. I made a small box for him to carry his merchandise in. The cotton gin was quite near our camp. Charles took the parched peanuts and occasionally bags of popcorn. I did not do this out of necessity, but it was something for him to do, which really boosted his ego and also was the beginning of his having some responsibility of his own.

MARY'S CONVICTION

When Mary was about seven or eight years of age, she had a pretty ring. It was a simple band with hearts on each side front. It was getting tight on her finger. So, she told the Lord if he didn't want her to wear rings, he could just take it off her finger. That very day, she lost the ring. The children were riding in the back of the watermelon truck which had hay on the bottom to protect the melons. She assumed she lost it in the truck. She never found it. She told me recently that was the reason for her never wearing or wanting a ring.

CHARLES GETS A SPANKING

Mary related to me recently that she never remembered her Daddy whipping any of the children except one time. She did not know what Charles had done to deserve a whipping, but their dad pulled off his belt and hit him two or three times and Cecil's pants fell off. They were in the backyard of our home.

MARY GOT INTO QUICKSAND

Cecil was trapping. We had gone with him on this particular day to run his traps. The children and I were sitting in the car, and I had just related to the children about my getting stuck in a 'suck hole'. That was what they called them when I was little.

Mary, Linda, and Charles got out of the car and wandered down to the small creek and guess what? Mary got into the little stream of water and down she went to her knees. She screamed and Charles got a big, long stick and put it down deep in the creek bed. She managed to pull herself out with Charles' help and the stick. She hasn't forgotten it.

CHARLES SELLING GRIT PAPERS

When Charles was about twelve years of age, he got him a Grit paper route. He would come in from school and, on a certain day, he took his papers to his customers. Charles rode a bicycle and went over on Christian Street or in that area to deliver papers. He was attacked by a bad, mean dog. The dog actually pulled him off his bicycle, tearing his clothes as well as his leg badly. This dog was kept tied, but for some reason had gotten loose. The fact that it was some of our friends' dog, we did not press any charges. I did go to the mother's place of employment and reported the dog being loose.

MARY GOT A SPANKING AT AGE 18

Mary had a boyfriend. Most everyone did at this age, but this boy was in and out of church all the time. He was an overbearing kind of person as a young man. I felt that, by the leading of the Spirit, he was not the one for her. After her dad's death, he became more persistent about wanting Mary to go ahead and marry him. I think she knew in her heart that I was right. But love, whether it's real love or puppy love, is blind. I guess she had broken up with him, gave him her decision, but she had not told me all of her mind. So, she cried and cried and would not tell me what was wrong. So, I whipped her. I don't know if I was right or not, but due to the circumstances at that time, I thought I did the right thing.

CHARLES WENT VISITING

When Charles was about eighteen months old, Mom and Dad were living near Chireno in Mrs. Nena Posey's house. Her house, at that time, was directly across the highway from Mr. and Mrs. Ragland's home. Charles went across the highway out to Mrs. Ragland's without any pants or diaper on. Mrs. Ragland brought him back and thought nothing of the matter. Mrs. Ragland was a very nice, articulate lady. She was also a very friendly neighbor. This lady was Johnny Ragland's grandmother. Johnny was in a band with my brother, Jesse.

CHARLES AND BAND

Charles was in the marching band most all of his high school years. He played the tuba. He loved the band, probably too much, but I did not know how he was feeling inside. The biggest problem, I think, was when they had to go off on the busses to the ball games away from home.

One morning Charles did not want to go to school. He would not tell me what was wrong. I asked him repeatedly and he would not give me an answer. I gave him a whipping and then he opened up with me.

He told me, "Mom, I am convicted going to the ball games." I suspected also what was going on there and back on the busses. At any rate, he did not think he could get out at that time. He only had six more weeks for his credit of that year in band. I told him, "Well, just go to the high school and march in that office and ask the principal." I believe the principal was Mr. Sullivan. Charles and I went to his office, and I explained as he had told me. Mr. Sullivan told him, "This is no problem. You just kind of keep quiet about getting out." He told Charles that he had plenty of credits to graduate as he would anyway.

Years later, I heard that this same man, Mr. Sullivan, received the Holy Ghost and was working for the Lord. My sister-in-law told me this. She had talked to him. I have often wondered if my going to talk to him concerning Charles, had any influence on him receiving the Holy Ghost.

MARY BURNS HER FEET

We were at Lockney, Texas. Mary always loved my shoes. I had carried one pair of dress shoes out there with me. She put them on and went out there behind our cabin and walked out into the huge pile of hot ashes where they burned the cotton burrs. It burned her feet badly, at least it looked that way. My mom's brother, Uncle Carter Hooper, lived there and he asked me, "Do you have some Irish potatoes?" I did have some. He had us scraping the potatoes as fast as we could and then replacing them again and again on her feet. It caused no serious burns.

A TRIP WITH CHARLES

When Charles and LaNelle moved to Haltom City, he was in the mobile home business, as he is even now. LaNelle was working at the office of National. I was visiting them and had been there by myself every day. The children were in school.

Charles asked me one night if I'd like to go with him the next day. He explained that he was going to pick up a new home from the factory. You see, I didn't think I'd ever find myself in that huge truck, with him pulling a long mobile home. This particular one was called an energy home that had thick walls and very, very heavy home. He assured me that there would be no danger what-so-ever. I spent a restless night praying, asking the Lord to take care of us and let me be ready to die, just in case.

We left long before daylight. Charles believes in getting things done in a hurry. Before we got to the plant, it had rained a lot. The parking lot was flooded with water. They did not have the home ready to go at the appropriate time. He had to wait for an hour or so. Finally, he pulled it out. As we got started, I noticed Charles kept looking in his rear-view mirror. I asked, "Is something wrong?" He said there wasn't. A few miles farther, he told me, "The trim is coming loose on the top of this home." He considered turning around and going back to the plant, but you don't turn a rig like that just anywhere. He could not find a place to turn around. Therefore, Charles started slowing down, thinking perhaps that would help but it kept coming loose more and more.

The problem wasn't that he couldn't fix the trim himself, but the problem was he had no way to get on top of the home. As a matter of fact, he stopped once and no way could he reach to the top. I was really praying in my heart by now because he had to fix it. He said, "If I have to block this two-lane highway, I've got to fix that trim because it could cause the top to lift also.

As Charles pulled to a stop, half on the highway, I looked up ahead and saw some 55-gallon barrels in a pasture. There was a gate he could open. I told Charles, "Look out there at those barrels." He went out and got one. He still had to do lots of stretching, but he was able to put screws into the top of that trim on one long side of the home. I told him, "The Lord provided these barrels." You see, he had driven for miles and miles going quite slowly. We talked about God's goodness to us.

EDWARD WAS A PERFECT TRAVELER

Edward, being my baby, got to go along with Cecil and I most of the time of his dad's life, that is to say the time he was able to work. We went all over to Paris, TX, South Texas, Oklahoma, and Florida buying hay, produce and watermelons. I made a bed in the floorboard of the truck and Edward would sleep there. When he awakened, he would look out the window and see the things of interest to him. He went many thousands of miles, and I don't recall him ever wanting to stay home. He was a good child and traveling did not upset him. Cecil installed a nice light in the truck that hung down and let us have light for traveling purposes. He just clicked a switch to turn it on.

LINDA AFRAID OF HORSES

When Linda was small, she had a terrible fear of horses. Mr. Gilis, who lived on Westview, would go peddling in his wagon. Mr. Gilis was married to Sister Brooksie Fitzgerald's sister. The older children delighted in telling Linda, "I see Mr. Gilis coming." In the house she came, screaming. I was always afraid of animals, so I know how she felt.

EDWARD AND LINDA PLAYING TOGETHER

Edward and Linda always played together so very well. They did not argue or fuss at all. They enjoyed it. Then as they got older, they still enjoyed each other. They would laugh and giggle and I would not see anything funny. Sometimes, I'd tell them, "I'd rather see you all this way than arguing."

EDWARD AND HIS TINKERTOYS

We got Edward a large can of Tinker toys. My, could he build things out of them. I said then and there that he would probably be a carpenter or at least like to make things. Edward did do this in the way of craft things for several years. Debbie was also so very good with the big saws and shop tools. Then Debbie was an excellent painter. I always appreciated you helping Edward to make extra money.

EDWARD WENT TO BUY HIM A VEHICLE

One day, I was working at the egg house near Jackson, MS. We lived there, of course. A man called me and asked me if he could come out there for me to sign some papers for my son, Edward. I said, "Would you explain, please?" He told me Edward was buying a car. I assured him that we could not buy the car at this time. I was used to him going to look at cars all the time, but he'd never gone that far. I suspect that the salesman had a big hand in taking it that far.

CHARLES RUNNING FROM ME

Charles was the hyper one. He would run from me when I would call him. Even if he knew he'd get a spanking. One day, we were over at Pinky Ma's when she lived on Westview. Big Girl lived up the road but there was a curve on the road. It was dangerous for children to be in the road. Charles had wanted to go to Big Girl's, so he was going up the road. I called and called him. He saw me, but would not stop, ran all the faster. He did get a spanking that day.

CHARLES AND HIS BUSINESS

It's almost a pattern or piece of a puzzle being fitted together for you, Charles, to love to do that truck driving like your dad. I know it's hard work and long house. I appreciate LaNelle helping you so much with your business when she could. I know long ago it was hard for her with you being gone so much, as well as it being hard on you.

EDWARD HOSPITALIZED FOR TONSILLECTOMY

Edward was probably about twelve years of age when we decided to go ahead and let Dr. James G. Taylor remove his tonsils. He was sick so much with this problem. In fact, he was sick when he entered the hospital. He kept getting worse and worse, finally breaking out in a very red rash. When the doctor came in one morning, I called his attention to the rash. He told me, "I'm pretty sure it's scarlet fever and you'll have to put him in isolation." He asked me to bring the other children up to his office and he'd give them a shot also. The girls were already sick. Dr. Taylore told me, he'd come out to my car and give the girls the injection, which he did.

Charles was a big boy and in the band classes that summer and I did not take him. He said, "It's unlikely he'll take it." But he did take it. He wasn't nearly as bad as the other children. Mary and Linda did have it regardless of the injections. Needless to say, Edward had to come home and wait about six weeks and then go back for his tonsillectomy. Edward would not let the nurses give him a shot unless I was there in his room.

CECIL'S VETERAN'S CHECK

Cecil was discharged with 30% disability. This was because of his hearing being impaired in the service (U.S. Army).

I have said before that Cecil was an honest person. Actually, he was very honest. He would do something that displeased me and then tell me about it. I had a businessman tell me one day that "Cecil was the most honest person he had ever had any dealings with." Cecil sold produce on a regular basis to this man.

I said all the above to say this. Cecil got a veteran's check every month, in the amount of $55.00 per month. Many times, he would tell me that he didn't want the check. So, one month, (actually, I think he did this twice) he sent it back and told me that he did not get the check. We had a post office box at the time. The Veteran's Administration sent the checks back. It was hard for him to accept help from any source.

'CECIL' MY HUSBAND

Cecil was a loving, kind, and considerate person. He was also a very nervous person. His first job there at Houston was in the shipyard firing a boiler. His boss said he was the most nervous person he'd ever seen.

We did not stay there at Galena Park very long, we moved on to Beaumont. I do not remember what job he had there.

Cecil was a very particular man when he was young. He had all his clothing and shoes matched. He soon bought me some pretty dresses to wear that matched his clothing.

Cecil had hazel eyes, brown hair, ruddy complexion. He liked to cook and also, he loved my cooking. He was an Army cook in the South Pacific. He was stationed on the Island of New Caledonia.

Cecil was an honest person. He primarily was a truck owner and driver. He owned a short-wheel-base truck and an 18-wheeler at the same time. He bought several new trucks. I remember Dad telling Cecil that his dad told him that "A debt made a good work monster."

Dad was instrumental in Cecil getting better. We spent most of our married life quite happy – just ordinary things that families encounter that was frustrating.

Cecil and Dad became very good friends. Also, Uncle Jesse Lee thought lots of Cecil, as did Grandpa Lee. Uncle Jesse said of Cecil "If he fell into a pit toilet, he would come out smelling like roses." Uncle Jesse often came over to our house and would come in and set down and get still, then fall asleep. He was not well at the time. He liked Cecil.

OCCUPATION

Cecil was a work-alcoholic. I am too. Age has changed me some. Cecil loved to work. He would be on the road for a day or two at a time and get home at 2:00 a.m., then sleep 3 or 4 hours and be ready to go again.

Cecil farmed the first year we were married. For the life of me, I don't recollect about the cotton or corn, but I do know that we had a fabulous garden.

Thereafter, he had trucks and worked for himself primarily. He and Dad did raise a watermelon crop one year. It was a sight to see that watermelon field. Many went to waste because they could not harvest them all.

Cecil bought and sold watermelons and hay. He made a good living doing this. I traveled with him over several states and many miles. So did Edward.

It seemed like Cecil thought there was dignity in toil, whether it was in the toil of his hands or toil of his head. All his labor seemed to supply his wants, make him happy, and in a sense elevate his own nature. I mean to say, all labor that is honest, is honorable too. I believe he thought that.

Dr. James G. Taylor told Cecil and I one day in his office "Cecil, I'd rather sit here and talk to you than all those people who stand on the streets in Nacogdoches and doesn't care one way or another if they ever work." Dr. Taylor told him. "It is smart people like you who lose it." He had much respect for Cecil.

HOBBIES

Cecil loved to fish, and he was one of the best in Nacogdoches County. He worked at this fishing like he did his labor for money.

I went along with him to the river many, many days. He used P&G soap cut up into little 1" squares to bait his fishhooks with. He caught channel catfish on this, not too big, not over 3 or 4 lbs. He used live bait, small perch, and small fish. He would sometimes have a 5 gallon can of crawfish for bait.

Cecil put out trot lines, sometimes he would have out 60 or 70 or more. Each line had 10 – 15 hooks per line. I have seen him take off several fish per line, and many times a 10- or 12-pound op. This was a yellow catfish, being the best fish there is to eat (my opinion).

Then Cecil fished with hoop nets. He bought them for some time, then he went to see Mom's first cousins to get them to teach him to tie the nets himself. This got to be a big thing for him. He was a whiz at doing this. He learned how to make a complete net in one day. The net fishing made him quite a bit of money. He did this with 'all his might'.

He believed to enjoy life was to have something to do. His life was full of constant work, which was what made him feel safe and happy.

Trapping for furs to sell was also his hobby. Well, not exactly a hobby. This was for a means of making money, too. He was a fantastic trapper. He diverted all his energy into this when he was engaged in trapping.

We lived at the little house down toward Etoile that Cecil had bought. It was in the deep forest. I hated it. Charles was a baby, and I might say, a big baby. There were lots of varmints in the woods on our place and in front of our house. Cecil had access to some good places to trap. The foxes barked so loud and furious at night that it frightened me terribly. I actually thought that they could come up to the house and get Charles. Anyway, my complaining prompted Cecil to trap for them. He plowed a ditch around our field and set his traps in the furrow. The next day he left early before day to go to his traps. He would usually be back by 10:00 a.m. but not so this day. Finally, I took Charles and dressed him for warmth and set out across the field to find him. I was sure he had crawled thru a fence and his gun gone off and killed him. I was furious. I walked a long way and finally saw him coming. He had caught so many foxes, that he had to skin them before coming home. All was well.

When Charles was a baby, we rented an old farmhouse down the lane from Mr. Roy Atkinson. We only stayed there 3 or 4 weeks. It came a bad cloud one night and was very stormy. To be accurate, it shook the house, so we got up in the fireplace before we decided to go to the storm cellar. We knew where it was but had never looked inside it. The thing was knee deep in water, but it had a platform made in it. We got on that. We were nearly as scared there (snakes) as we were of the wind.

The next morning Cecil could not get to any of his traps because of high water, so he went to Nacogdoches. It had come a storm at Nacogdoches that night and I know that it blew away several houses on Seale St. Mr. and Mrs. Pinkston lived on that street, but it had missed their home. We were thankful.

This particular year, he caught about 20 minks on one particular log in front of our house. He got $30.00 each for the mink that year.

Back to net fishing. I have been in the 14' flat bottom boat with Cecil many times, running his hoop nets. He would often catch a boat full in just a couple of nets. These were 'buffalo' scale fish. He had license to sell them, which he did.

This was quite expensive to make a net. He first bought nylon thread or twine to tie one, then came the making of it. Then he bought a greenish-black stuff to treat the nets with. This preserved them and made them last a long time. I might say here that he kept the nets in the water a few days at a time, then took them up, and dried and repaired them.

Next on making the nets, he hooped them. Sometimes he gathered grape vines and made the hoops. These hoops had advantages and disadvantages. The advantage being, they did not show up in the water as being anything unusual. The disadvantage was, they were easily broken as they were taken out of the water (full of fish). Therefore, he mostly bought metal tubing and made his hoops.

Most every year, Cecil would catch a big yellow catfish. Sometimes he dressed the fish and put it into the freezer, but he was most likely to sell them. There was always a demand for the big fish. This brought him a little extra ready money.

I recall one day he came home with a big fish, and he said "I'm gonna take this to the school and show the children." They were in high school, which today is the junior high school located on Mound Street here in Nacogdoches, TX. He took the fish and many of the children's classmates and teachers came out to see it. It would have weighed 50 or 60 lbs.

THE TRUE GENTLEMAN

A gentleman is a man who is gentle. I am so sorry that Cecil was a sick person and thus did not live a longer life with us. He was a tender, loving person. He loved me and his children.

Until Cecil became so ill and was unable to cope with life, he was a very good husband and father.

He called his children 'babies'. Once he went into a motel to rent a room and told them he had 4 babies. When we got to the room, we had two baby beds, plus our bed.

Cecil was a man of his word. If he told someone, he would do something, they could depend on it.

Until the day he died, he would come to my car and carry in my groceries or whatever. He always depended on me to pay the bills. He always gave me spending money, pretty well let me do as I wanted to do. He carried out the garbage on a regular basis.

He was a man of just principles, love in his heart for me, and sympathy for the underprivileged. Many a time, I've seen him give the fish he had caught to someone whom he thought needed them. Then I've witnessed him stopping on the road and giving children money to go and get them an ice cream cone.

Cecil did not have more than a grammar school education, but he had a large fund of 'five senses' and lots of 'common sense'. He liked to read good books when he had time.

He applied the education he had with lots of painstaking effort. He lived according to what he knew as far as goodness was concerned. It was not by accident that Cecil was able to do as well as he did, in the time we were married, but rather he had great purpose and was very persistent in making a go of his life.

I wish all of you grandchildren and great-grandchildren could have known your Grandfather Cecil.

Cecil thought the first step toward greatness was to be honest. He was probably right. He always gave people 'good measure, heaped up, and running over' in his produce dealings.

Back then, many people bought groceries 'on credit'. Cecil bought a few bills of groceries 'on credit' our first year of marriage but only a few. He always paid cash for whatever he bought, with the exception of his trucks and cars.

Cecil was a person slow to anger; a lot more so than I was. I've heard said 'always have a good stock of patience laid by and be sure you put it where you can find it.' I think Cecil possessed patience, generally speaking, much more than I did, but then I minded everything at home mostly by myself. Guess that's no excuse.

Cecil was a loving person. I really believe that he did love me. In fact, the last time I went to the hospital, (V.A. Veteran's Administration) and got him 2 weeks prior to his death, he told me on the way home "It is so good for us to be together again." "This is the way I want it to always be." "I want us to live together and die together." Incidentally, Laverne was with us that day.

Cecil told me many times that "I love you more now than I ever did." The affection that put us together as man and wife got to be a far holier and more enduring passion than the enthusiasm of our young love.

Cecil and I lived for many years a very happy life. It was not boring at all. He wanted me to be with him in doing whatever he was doing. I went in the trucks with him many miles over many states. After he was disabled and fished a lot, I went with him on the boat fishing for 6 hours or so a day. Then he helped me in the home, canning, tying quilts, cooking, or whatever we were doing at the time.

Cecil was a generous person, but he was also just. He would not give away what did not belong to him. He was sure he could pay for a truck when he bought one.

He surely would have been amazed at how people live today, on every hand we see people living on credit, putting off payday to the last, making some effort to get one more payment together to pay one more time on a 'Visa' or 'Mastercard'. In reality they're only paying interest.

He believed that we ate and drank this month what he earned last month, not what he was going to earn next month.

I titled this 'a true gentleman'. I've tried to name a few things that I believe denoted a gentleman in Cecil. He was polite, he did not talk down to nobody. He was not greedy. If he borrowed, he went to a bank, and never troubled friends or relatives with his troubles.

RESPECT AND LOVE

I do not mean to be disrespectful to Cecil, our children, or even the Pinkston name. Some of my grandchildren asked me many years ago about their grandfather as to why he died at such an early age. They have wanted to know more about him in general. I thought it would be best if I told them myself as I saw him.

You all keep in mind that I knew him as a young man when his health was fine, he was a very good-looking young man. In other words, I loved him, long before you all were born.

I don't mean to sound harsh about Cecil, in some of the things I have related in this book. Also, I want you all to know he had some weaknesses, some traits that were not perfect, but I did not dwell on those things then, neither do I now. I have not written any degrading thing about your Dad or Granddaddy. I have many faults and am not a perfect person either.

Love is such that it expels things that are ugly and base. It makes us think of the good there is in a person. Love illuminates our paths when they are the darkest.

When someone gets to the point of despair and has lost all hope, that's when Satan tells them they can't go on. A strong mind always hopes and has always cause to hope.

Hope awakens courage, while despondency is the last straw. The giving up of the battle of life with nothingness.

I have read the last letters this week of March 12, 1995, that Cecil wrote to me and the children. It made me sad, restless, and sleep would not come. He certainly was a sick man but still expressing his love to me, and his family. I did not go to Houston with him to stay, the last time he was hospitalized. The children were in school and to tell the truth, I needed some rest. He called often and I went to see him often on weekends.

It has been hard for me to write the things down on paper that has been inside me for so long.

I trust that my children and all their families will always know that Jesus is the answer to life's problems. I don't mean to imply that you won't have problems, because we will all always have problems and trials as long as we live, but with Jesus in us, He helps us bear them and it does make a difference.

We think so many times that we know whom God approves of and who he doesn't, but I'm afraid that oftentimes we view things under a false sight, and thus pass our judgements accordingly. God is the one who really knows everyone and judges us from our hearts.

Cecil had principle, love, and honesty. His life was made up of little courtesies, little kindnesses, good wishes, and good deeds. I can't remember a time in our married life that Cecil didn't have any money. He also saw that I always had spending money or more. He depended on me to pay all the bills and attend to business matters primarily.

So, children, please never be cast down by misfortunes. Our own mistakes and errors many times teach us more than precepts of others.

It's more important to aspire after things you love to do, rather than money or that which someone else desires for you. Happiness is the key and God is the answer.

MY VERY FIRST TRIP TO THE V.A. HOSPITAL AT HOUSTON WITH CECIL

I had known for some time that I had to get Cecil in the Veteran's Hospital. I was driving everywhere but I didn't have a driver's license. Things were so bad at home with him, so I really started praying and fasting about us going to Houston.

I didn't know anyone there and I wasn't sure they would hospitalize him that first time. We were there all day, seeing one doctor and then the other. It was after dark and one person had told me, they did not have a bed for him at that time. We started down the hall and another doctor came behind us and said, "You wait. This man is service-connected, and we have got to get him a bed." So, they did.

I had dreamed about this place before I went down there. It was a big, old, house and inside it had antique furniture. Also, there were stacks and stacks of books and magazines all over the house. That night after Cecil was committed to the hospital, I started calling people who had their phone numbers at the social services there at the hospital. I was at the bottom of the list when I called and this lady said, "Why, yes, you come on out here and I'll find you a bed." This lady's name was Mrs. Miller. When I walked in the house, this was the place I had dreamed about in every respect.

This place was close enough to the hospital that I walked to and from with other people who had patients at the V.A. also and were staying there. Mrs. Miller let me make quilts and quilt them for her for my rent. She also insisted I bring my children there in the summer and I did.

Jesus, you were so good to me then, as well as now.

152

WHEN WE LIVED AT MRS. MILLER'S ON BINZ AT HOUSTON

I had the children with me all summer one year while Cecil was in the V.A. Hospital. The boys got quite a few jobs around in the area, cleaning people's yards. I remember them cleaning off the roofs of some homes. We had to have money to buy our food we ate. I worked for Mrs. Miller making some quilt tops and then I quilted several quilts for her. This paid our room rent.

There was a couple staying at Mrs. Miller's that had two daughters who could neither speak nor hear. They were from Victoria, Texas. They came to Houston to have their little girls seen by doctors. Mary babysat for them quite a bit. Then one day, they wanted to go to the zoo. The mother of the children asked Mary to go and help her with her children. She went and that afternoon, the lady gave Mary $50. She was so happy because I needed gas money badly at the time. Mary knew that the Lord had helped her to get this job.

MARY'S PRAYER ANSWERED

During this time that we were in Houston, Mary said she had wanted a blue, striped, seersucker skirt. I sewed for the girls all the time and made them what I thought was pretty clothes to wear. They laughed later and told me, "All the things we ever got new were sweaters and coats," and that was because I couldn't make these.

Mary was praying for this particular color and material. Someone brought a big box of clothing to Mrs. Miller's and there was a blue, striped, seersucker skirt and for good measure, a pink one also, and they fit her. She's never forgotten this prayer answered for her. Also, she mentioned some man bringing boxes of donuts there every week and giving them to her. Mary is still depending on the Lord, and he's never failed her yet.

ONE RAINY NIGHT

Cecil was in the hospital at this time. Mary, Linda, and I went as far as Diboll and spent the night with LaVerne, Aubry and family. I did this many times so I would not have to get up so early. We left there about 3:00 A.M. It was raining a slow rain all the way.

I was traveling on down the road. I believe Mary was in the front seat with me. All of a sudden, she said, "Mama, watch, there's a man in the road." I had not seen him until she spoke. He was not only in the road, but in the middle of my side of the road. I barely missed the man. There were two other men, also. He yelled something we couldn't understand. There was no car in view anywhere. In fact, there wasn't room to park a car in that area.

It really excited us. I drove at least 80 miles an hour until I got to Cleveland. Then we thought it was safe for us to stop, take a breather, and get refreshed. We never told Cecil about this. It would have upset him badly.

CECIL LEAVES HOSPITAL WITHOUT A PASS

Cecil was under heavy medication as well as taking shock treatments. Charles and I were the only ones staying at Mrs. Miller's at this time. This was a rooming house just for people who had relatives staying in the nearby hospitals.

The other three children were at Brother and Sister Lamon's at Lufkin. Mary and Linda both were very much on fire for God at this time and I think they spent all the available time they had at the Lamon's church praying, which was next door to their home. I appreciated Sister Lamon keeping the children for me at that particular time.

Charles and I went to visit Cecil morning and evening, or at least talked to him. This time was a Friday afternoon that we went, he walked to the car with us, then told me to "Move over, he was going home." This was a nightmare. It was the time of day that traffic was heavy, and Cecil was afraid someone was following him, and should not have been driving at all, because of his medications. He would drive right up so fast to the cars, sometimes he'd have to get off the road. He refused to let Charles or myself drive.

Mary had had a vision about us and was praying at the church for 9 hours, because she knew we were in trouble. I had called the day before and told Sis. Lamon we were not coming home because Cecil had to get a shock treatment that Friday.

Mary saw a vision of a car sliding off the road and rocks flying. She went and told Sister Lamon that we were coming home. She said "No, Mary, Hazel called yesterday and said we were not coming."

It wasn't too long before we drove up. Perhaps if Mary, Linda, and Shirley had not been in prayer about all day, we might have had that wreck.

GOING TO PINKY PA & PINKY MA'S AT THE RIVER

The very next day, after Cecil leaving the hospital without permission, he decided we'd all go to his mom and dad's. They were sorta camping at the Attoyac River fishing. They had a house rented there at the time.

So, I told him "We'll go, but let Charles drive." He told me he could drive, but he had all of us to get in the car, then he came out of the house with the shotgun getting in the front seat with him.

On the way down there, it was quite early, around eight o'clock. We passed the county barn, and I noticed all the men were getting in their trucks to leave for work. Hershel, my brother, worked for the county, thus driving a truck. A short distance from the county barn, Cecil said "Stop this car, there's a bomb under the hood." I immediately thought about those trucks coming right behind us and I knew Hershel would stop. Anyway, Charles pulled off the road, jumped out, so did he, and so did I get out and raised the hood and told him "Look there's no bomb under there." Then, I helped him get back in the car as quickly as I could, closed his door, ran back, and got back in the car, and Charles got away as fast as he could. The trucks were very near us.

Mr. and Mrs. Pinkston were glad we came. They really didn't know the severity of Cecil's health, up until this day.

Mr. Pinkston was sitting on the porch and Cecil went outside and actually attacked him. I had to talk to him, reasoning with him to try to get him settled down.

I got on the phone there and called the hospital, telling them the circumstances and asking if I could bring him back. I had to talk to several different people, and I believe make 2 calls. Now this was just the 'first' step for me to take. I did not know 'how' I was going to get him back down there. They gave me instructions as to how to go about it. I would have to use the same procedure as if he had never been admitted to the hospital.

So, I started asking Cecil "If he would go back to the hospital.". It wasn't an easy task. This was one time I was depending on God's help, asking in His Name, and believing. I told him "I'll leave the boys home this time. Linda and Mary would like to go down there and stay a few days with me." So finally, Cecil said he'd go but he was going to drive.

He carried a book with him and tried to read it while he was driving. I was on the front seat, Mary and Linda were on the back seat of the car. As we crossed the old bridge over the San Jacinto River going into Houston, he suddenly pulled off the road and we though he was headed down into the great blue yonder, but he stopped. I talked to him a little and he calmed down but would not let me drive. It was getting near dark.

I kept asking him to let me drive before we got downtown. That was the route he took, down Main Street, Houston. When he came to this red light, he stopped suddenly, jumped out, and ran around the car. We thought he was going to run off, but he didn't. One of girls opened the door for him. He got in the back seat with Mary and Linda got in the front seat with me.

I drove on to the hospital. They would not let the girls go any further than the front waiting room. They had to stay there. As a matter of fact, it took quite some time for me to get him admitted.

After we got in the car going out to Mrs. Miller's, Mary told me, "Mama, Daddy put his pocketknife in his sock when he got in the back seat." Due to the fact he was not supposed to have it and since he had jumped on patients there before, it was important for me to call the hospital and report this. This was at least midnight or later by now. I called the hospital. They told me "You cannot talk on that ward at this time of night." But after I explained they were happy to let me talk to someone.

Needless to say, they searched him and took the knife. He told me about it the next day, never knowing that Mary told me.

TIME FOR FASTING AND PRAYING

It seemed as if I prayed day and night when Cecil was so sick. I fasted one time ten days without eating a bite, and Cecil never even noticed. What he did notice though, was my praying. We had made an upstairs out of our attic. It was quite big and nice. We had a double bed plus a little half bed up there. This was the boy's bedroom.

I would go up there and pray, sometimes for an hour or so. One such day, Cecil came up there. I felt this same feeling of fear as I've mentioned in other topics. He asked me if I'd like to lay down awhile. So, we did on the small bed, that's what he suggested.

After his death, I found shells for his 45 between those mattresses. I don't know if he had any intention of doing anything up there or not.

WHEN I REALLY GOT SCARED

The children were all in school or perhaps Charles might have been working. Cecil and I were in our bedroom, and I do not remember what our conversation was, but I had answered him in the wrong way, tone, or something. He pushed the bedroom door closed and grabbed me around the throat and choked me very badly. I really thought he was going to kill me then.

When I could get away, I ran out to Pinky Ma and told her what had happened, and I was afraid to go back in the house. I went in her back bedroom and went to bed, stayed there all day. Cecil came out and talked to them later but did not come in where I was. After the children got home, I went back. To this day, my throat is affected from that.

LINDA AND MARY SEEING A LIGHT

One night, not very many days before Cecil took his life, a strange thing happened. Linda and Mary came in from church one night. I did not go this particular night. I was in bed asleep. Shortly after they came in, coming into the kitchen which had the front door, they had not turned on the lights, just trying to be quiet. Right after they'd come in and closed the door there was a long, bright light that shone across from that kitchen door. It scared them nearly to death.

They didn't want to awaken me, so Mary called Sister Carrie Minton, our pastor. She told her about the light and asked her what it meant. Sis. Minton said, "Sister Mary, I don't know, but sometimes seeing a light indicates a death soon." Mary had the date and incident written in her diary, but somewhere she lost or left a box of her treasures of yesteryear.

Incidentally, this was the exact spot that Cecil took his life, actually falling straight across at the place they had seen the light.

THE WEEK BEFORE THE TRAGEDY

On Friday night before this tragic Sunday, Linda, Edward, and I went to Mom and Dad's to spend the night. Every once in a while, I would need to get away. Just going down there helped me.

Mary didn't want to go, because her girlfriend had confided in her that she had planned to leave school that Friday with a guy to get married without consent from her mom. Mary was interested in perhaps learning something more concerning Lois.

She had to go into her dad's bedroom to look out the window to view Lois' home. This seemed to disturb her dad. She said several times he got up and came through her bedroom (only way out) with the pistol in his pants. At one of these times, she said she was not asleep, but he stopped for a minute in her room, and it made her have an uneasy feeling. I have thanked God many times that he did not hurt her.

Cecil called me twice at Mom's that night telling me how much he loved me, and he said, "I've gained 10 lbs. since I've been home from the hospital, all because of your good cooking."

No one would have thought that Cecil was a kind of person to try and take my life and then take his own life, but it happened. They did not know how his mind was messed up. He strictly was fouled up, as a result of the service (U.S. Army). Although he was not on the firing line of battle, he was quite near the fighting.

Close enough to hear bullets and for the grass to catch fire on the particular place where his cooking tent was located. He was a cook.

On the ship going over, he spent 31 days and nights on it, the ship was torpedoed and knocked the people out of their bunks. He could not keep anything on his stomach day or night. He told me that someone told him to eat crackers and water and nothing else, and it did help him. It was on the ship over that his hearing was impaired, so he had to wear a hearing aid from then on. I prayed all the time he was in the service for him.

I had fasted many days, onetime 10 days prior to this tragedy. I prayed much and the Lord had given me many dreams. I knew the time was close and I was expecting him to take his own life, but I really didn't expect him to hurt me, until the last few months. The fact was that he wanted us to die together. He had said that in the car coming home from the hospital in Houston 2 weeks prior. He said to me, "This is so sweet of you to come after me. I just want us to live together and die together." I had forgotten him saying that, but Laverne reminded me of it.

BUYING KNIVES AT AN OUTLET STORE IN CENTER

Cecil and I went to this store occasionally. It was one of those places that had a little of everything. This time was during the last days he was home from the hospital, which was only 2 weeks prior to his death.

They had some sets of knives. These were several in a set, like carving knives or butcher knives. Cecil said, "Let's buy one set of these for you, and one for me." I told him we didn't need all those knives, but he bought them. I was suspicious of this.

The day that he tried to kill me and then took his life, we had all eaten lunch and Mr. and Mrs. Pinkston, as well as my children, except Edward, along with LaNelle and Sue, had gone to a funeral. Cecil asked me if I was going with them. I told him "No, I'm staying with you." Then after they left, he was standing with his back to the kitchen sink, and he had one of those butcher knives, holding it as if

160

to stab me. I had a sense of exactly what he was thinking. I said to him, "Come on, honey, let's go lay down and rest." So, he laid the knife down.

THE TRAGIC DAY

This tragic day was on Sunday, November 1, 1964. I had cooked lunch before I went to church. I had a pie or something to finish when I got back. Cecil asked me could I fix lunch today. I told him I had it almost prepared.

When we got in, he was out at his mom and dad's next door (Pinky Ma & Pinky Pa). He came on out. He told me "I've already eaten with Mama, but I'll eat with y'all, too." And he did.

The children, all except Edward, were going to Mr. Sam Montgomery's mother's funeral.

We went into our bedroom and went to bed. We had two regular size beds we slept on. He on one, me on the other. He was very restless. I knew he was not asleep. I got up once and went into the kitchen to get a drink, back to bed. I lay there quite a while longer. He probably thought I was asleep. He got up and when he did, he dropped the heavy long-handled claw hammer on the floor, which was concrete slab and had tile on it. It made a terrible noise, I rolled over and stood up, and when I did, he hit me on the head with the hammer, knocked me down across the bed, splattered blood all the way on the wallpaper across the bed. I don't know if he hit me more than once or not.

I wrestled with him to get the hammer away from him, at the same time, I was screaming for Edward. He was out at the back of the house with Dwayne Ward building something. My hands and arms were blue to my elbows.

161

I finally got out of the room, thru the house and outside and I called Edward again. He came running and saw me with my head bleeding. He started toward his Daddy. I said "Edward, don't do that. Dad has hurt Mama." Edward said, "Dad's got the gun." I didn't know he had gone to his mom's and gotten them. I had carried all of them out there. I told Edward to lay down on the ground and he did.

Cecil came to the gate and started firing the gun. I believe the second shot hit me thru my right side and this bullet had to be removed. Then he fired toward Edward 2 or 3 times. I ran to the tree and got behind it. He fired 2 shots into the tree and then came out to the road, put the gun up to my left shoulder and fired. This bullet went thru and thru the bone. Then I turned and he shot across my back, top shoulder. This bullet went in and out. This emptied his gun of 7 rounds.

He walked back and put the gun up to his head and said, "Look here." I said "Honey, don't do that!" The gun being empty, he had to reload it, so Edward jumped over the fence and went that way. I ran down the road.

We saw Charles, Mary, Linda, and all the others coming. I'll never forget how I felt for all of them to see me, including his mom and dad. We got in the car, Charles took me to the hospital, which I didn't think I wanted to go. I told him "Take me to Sister Minton's." but he said "No!" By the time I got there to the hospital, my arm and leg was numb.

I had dreamed one night of that week, that I was walking in his tracks, and he was in muddy water going down. I just know the Lord was trying to show me something.

When the shot went thru my stomach, I thought "Well, this is it. I will die." Then I thought about the scripture I had read and re-read. "If God be for us, who can be against us?"

Charles called the police and told them to go to our home, telling them the circumstances. They found Cecil dead.

Children, grandchildren, great grandchildren: I wish you could have known all I knew about him. He was sick, had lost all hope, and he loved me, wanted me to die with him. I went with him everywhere, many thousands of miles over many states but God was not ready for me to go with him to my grave.

I'm sorry, Mark, that Granny just couldn't tell you about this, when you asked me, you were about 10 years old. It's been hard for me to write this, but I wanted you all to know, he was not a brutal man.

I am thankful for my sweet, kind grandchildren that I have, now my great-grandchildren.

LOVE AND HOPE

These things I have related in these writings will not mean as much to whomever reads it as it has to me, because, you see, this is not just a life, but it's been exciting, sad, happy, and enjoyable because it is my life.

I feel that I have passed through times when I felt despair. This, too, has helped me to be more Christ-like.

As I wrote these episodes, there have been things brought to my mind, that I didn't particularly want to recall. At the same time, I need to accept them, and perhaps I can forget them.

We talk an awful lot about love, and I do believe we must love one another. The Bible speaks of being 'bound together with cords of love'.

I think another virtue that we neglect is 'hope'. People are so apt to think "What's the use?" We need to be always ready to say, "There's always hope." In Psalms 39:7 "My hope is in thee." In Colossians 1:27 "Christ in you, the hope of glory."

I have members of my family from age 2 years to 50. I'd like to think that each one of you will have one thing in common, that is to remember me by the kindness and wisdom I've tried to use through the years, and not the things I have done that wasn't so kind and, certainly I've missed the mark many times when it came to wisdom.

Parents with small children, you need to teach your children first of all about Jesus. I am thankful that most of you are doing that. As a general rule, I have found that our likes and dislikes do not change as we become an adult. If a child is taught that there is a Jesus, one who answers prayers and, if and when they make a mistake, ask him for forgiveness, then as they grow older, this will be a natural thing for them to do.

Children of today go to school and have things arranged for them and therefore they do not seem to produce any ideas of their own as to something to do.

If things are constantly being done to amuse you, naturally you expect it, and when nothing is done for you, you are at a loss. It's a pity to suffer from "nothing to do." Many women do. They suffer from loneliness and boredom.

We need to be able from a child to have an interest in something. I always liked 'sewing materials'. I have thru the years. Also, I have always loved to cook, and my interest hasn't changed. There are millions of talents more important, but what I'm saying, learn to create something for you to do. It will make a happy person out of you.

I do so appreciate all my children 'staying married'. I know life is full of hardships, but separations cause many more hardships.

Marriage is more than a lover. I believe respect is necessary. Respect is not to be confused with admiration. I think it would be very hard to feel admiration for a man all through one's married life. Respect is a thing that you don't have to dwell on, you just know thankfully it's there.

A woman wants to think that in her mate there is integrity. A person she can depend on in difficult times. There will be times when decisions have to be made, and a woman needs to feel secure, and respect her mate's judgement to handle everything.

A woman has the job of childbearing, child rearing, cooking, and homework. I know times has changed but this still remains true. This means keep house, it means there is no end to housework. Mom always said, "A man's work is from sun to sun, a woman's work is never done."

CHANGE

Sometimes we have to shift our living patterns and then it seems like we are all alone. I went through a great, drastic change when Cecil was no longer with us. It was an awful change for all the family. Then when my dad passed away, this was another great change for me. Dad had asked me to take care of Mom and Uncle Noah. Then there was Hershel's sudden death. I mention deaths ahead of my children marrying because these members of my family were very dependent upon me.

It's the will of God for changes. He intended for young people to marry and have children. Our seasons change each year from spring, summer, autumn and winter. We would get tired of having the same kind of weather all the time.

It is good for us to be able to change, therefore living each day fully as though it might be the last day there is. The only way we can change our yesterdays is to ask the Lord to forgive us, wherein we have failed in the past. I've done so many things I would do differently today, but yesterday is gone. We don't have the promise of tomorrow, but today is ours. Life is full of adjustments and there are no perfect situations.

If we could learn, and we can, to hold on to the happy moments while heading for the next hump. There have been many inventions over the years, but no one has invented a scale to measure a person's heart or the desires of the heart. Changes in a person's circumstances can bring about a change in one's attitude.

Living for the Lord is not an escape from life. It is the only means whereby, in all circumstances, with whatever life may bring, it is possible to be at peace in it.

But whatever the trials of life, whether it's death, sickness, financial problems, worry about our children, grandchildren, friends or whomever, we have to stop and remember that God is our very present help in time of trouble. Trust in the Lord is about the same as faith. God is greater than the World and all its problems.

I read this story about an art gallery where one certain painting didn't seem to attract any buyers. One day, someone re-hung the painting, placing it upside down, and doubled the price. Within a week, a customer came by, paid the asking price and bought it. I don't know if this was true or not but the message it illustrated to me, being that sometimes a simple solution often works by looking at it in a different view. Turning the problem around or upside down lets us see things differently.

WORK-A-HOLIC

People now-a-days call me a workaholic. If I am, I could have inherited it, or it was a result of observance and because of necessity. I just realized the need to work, thus being able to have more food, money, or whatever the need. The real truth of the matter being "I love to work". I enjoy it. I love long walks in the woods, country life, quiet, peace, and serenity that only God can give as we look to him.

MY HOSPITAL STAYS

1948 The first time I was ever a patient in a hospital (which was Memorial in Nacogdoches), was to give birth to Linda Faye Pinkston. This would have been May 13th, 1948.

1949 The next time was to give birth to Edward Earl Pinkston. This was December 30th, 1949, at Memorial Hospital in Nacogdoches.

1950 I went to Memorial Hospital probably later part of February 1950 to have the very first surgery of my life. I had to have a bladder suspension and I had a tubal.

1964 The next time was November 1st, 1964, when Cecil had hurt me and shot me 3 times. I stayed perhaps a week.

1964 I was only home from the hospital a few days and had pleurisy really bad from the "first rate infection" of the bullet through my stomach. I had to stay a few more days at Memorial.

1968 I went to Baptist Hospital when I lived in Jackson, MS., was there a short time for tests about 1968.

1973 I remember well that Debbie carried me to Doctor's Hospital. I remained here a day or two getting x-rays and tests. This too was at Jackson, MS. The doctor came in one night and said, "Little lady, we are going to have to cut on you." He proceeded to explain about the hiatal hernia and surgery was needed soon. I asked, "How soon". He said, "They'd do it the next day". I insisted they put it off until the following day so my family from Texas could be there. So, they did. This was in 1973. Dr. Netterville performed the surgery. After they came in the room and gave me the shot to kinda make you not care, I saw a scripture in the bible that actually illuminated. I spoke the scripture aloud. I wrote this down somewhere, but I've forgotten what it was.

1974 I had blood problems and was under the care of a Dr. Scheefer at Jackson. He had treated me for months. I could not eat, losing weight. Back to the hospital again. They sent me to University Hospital in Jackson this time. I was to remain there 3 weeks before surgery, for extensive testing. I had surgery for the removal of my spleen, also my gall bladder at the same time, plus Dr. Netterville opened up my esophagus again. (He had performed the hiatal hernia the year before.) This was in 1974.

I almost did not make it this time. I was very run-down, skin and bones. But the danger was my spleen was enlarged three times the size it should have been. I hemorrhaged very badly when they operated.

I was in surgery or recovery all day long. All the family were very disturbed. Sister Lamon came when I had this surgery, plus all my children and my mom, Dad, and sisters.

This experience was very real, I am going to relate. I rose above the bed, like I was suspended upward and could see all the doctors and nurses working frantically with me. I kept telling them "I am dying, I am hemorrhaging to death."

I was brought back to my room; I believe after dark. Mary and Elsie spent the night there that night with me.

I aroused sometime later just for a split second. I looked and I was on a heart monitor. I questioned that in my mind.

Mary said that all night long I mumbled "I am dying." "I am hemorrhaging to death." I had tubes everywhere. My bed would be soaked in blood every few hours, the tube could not contain the flow of blood. It was to be this way for the week. They were planning to take me back to surgery when the bleeding subsided some. My fever was 104 and much more all week.

All the family was concerned when I came out of recovery. My face was swollen. I had blood all over my face and on my hair. I know beyond a shadow, that my life did depart, when I had that vision, but God said again, "Not now."

1974 While I was in University Hospital the 3 weeks prior, they had discovered a tumor on my hip, inside the bone. Since I was unable to wait on myself, I decided to come home and stay with Mom and Dad for a while.

I went to see Dr. James G. Taylor, he examined me and sent me to Dr. Jorgensen. He had only been in Nacogdoches a short time. He took x-rays and told me he'd never done this type of surgery, but he knew something needed to be done. He took the tumor out, and then and there saw the shape my bones were in. This was quite painful afterwards.

I remember going to Dr. Jorgensen's office one day after surgery, my hip hurting me so badly. He sent one of his nurses out to the hospital to get a certain kind of needle. She had to return two or three times to get one large enough. In the meantime, they had prepared my hip for this mysterious thing he was fixing to do. He stuck that needle with all his strength (seemed like) into that hip, the blood came pouring out, all over the table and me. This was what it needed, but I almost fell out with him over that procedure.

Dr. Jorgensen's office at this time was across from the emergency entrance, where the parking lot is now. One of his sweet nurses, Cinda, was killed in a car wreck about this time. Jean Wells also worked for him. At this time, she's still a nurse, presently at Memorial in Emergency. This surgery was in 1974.

1974 As everybody knows, my bones are my greatest medical problem. I was not able to afford the prescription medications I needed for pain. (I thought I wasn't.)

I purchased me a bottle of aspirins from TexasT for 59 cents. Guess what? This caused the ulcer scars on my stomach to start bleeding, and this is terrific pain.

Dr. Taylor sent me to the hospital for tests. Dr. Cagle looked into my stomach and told me what he saw. I really had to buy medication then.

I remember this was at Thanksgiving time. My doctor had told me the day before, he'd let me out the next day, but he was slow coming in. Elsie and J.B. had come by to get me, but after them staying awhile, I told them to go on to Mom's and Dad's. She had Thanksgiving dinner for the family. They had just gotten there; my doctor came in and released me. Someone came back to get me. This was perhaps in 1974.

1975 Dr. Jorgensen saw me routinely until he performed a complete hip replacement in 1975. I asked him "Why he didn't put the complete hip in 6 months prior, when he had taken out the tumor?" He told me "He was trying to save my hip." This was the very worst pain I'd ever encountered. Bone surgery is different. There was no rehab at the hospital then, but my, how they worked with me, to teach me to walk. I went from the hospital to stay with Selvia for about 6 weeks. She was so very watchful of me when she was home. She was working full time, but she prepared all my meals for me to have everything by the couch, so I didn't need to move, only to go to the bathroom. Aunt Ella and Uncle Covy lived across the street. They checked on me also. I'd say that I made about 6 full size quilt tops by hand while I could not do anything else. I started piecing these while I was still hospitalized. Elsie cut out most of the blocks for me. I made Dr. Jorgensen a quilt.

1986 I had a bout with the flu and went to the emergency room. Dr. Henderson admitted me, saying I had some jaundice. I was there several days, in perhaps 1986.

1988 On June 13, 1988, I had one eye "implant" after cataract surgery. Only one day for this at Medical Center, Nacogdoches TX with Dr. Robert P. Lehmann.

1988 On August 8, 1988, I had cataract surgery on the other eye. One day in Medical Center, Nacogdoches, TX.

1991 Dr. Henderson sent me to the hospital to have a myelogram on my back. This was to be a simple thing to do, perhaps an overnight stay. The myelogram was a terrible ordeal for me and after I returned to my room, I became very nauseated each time I had to get up. They gave me Darvocet and I was allergic to that. I stayed in the hospital 5 days. Sis. Sherby came after me to bring me home. I was so sick on the way home. This was in 1991.

1991 In 1991, Dr. Samaratunga performed surgery to remove calcium deposit on or near a vertebra in my upper neck. Also, he did carpal tunnel surgery on my right hand at the same time.

1991 I had to wear the neck collar for some time, due to the neck surgery. The very day I took this off, my left jaw started hurting awful bad, I could hardly open my mouth. Dr. Samaratunga sent me to a Dr. Hurst on Raguet St in Nacogdoches, he works with facial problems. He performed a minor surgery on my jaw, finding the lining worn out, saying "It looks awful in there." All he could do at that time, was wash it out and pull the lining back between the bones. It's been hurting in both jaws recently. This was 1991.

1992 After I had the neck surgery, I had been confined to the couch quite a bit. My left shoulder started hurting me. The pain was so severe, I called Elsie at 2:00 in the morning. They carried me to the emergency room. Got a pain killing shot, back home. By the late afternoon, I had to go back to the emergency room, another high-powered shot. Monday morning found me in Dr. Henderson's office. He injected me with cortisone in the shoulder. By the later part of the week, I went to see Dr. Jorgenson, he x-rayed me, nothing broken, but he knew I was in severe pain.

This being the shoulder that I had the bullet go through and through the bone probably had something to do with the pain, although it had been years. Dr. Jorgenson sent me to the hospital. I had therapy for several days and they also had me wear one of those electric "tinge" machines. Everything that was done evidently distributed the pain, however it hurts all the time. This was 1992.

__1992__ In the year of 1992, on a Wednesday night, my face started hurting me in a different way than I'd ever had anything to hurt. This was on a Labor Day weekend. My illness progressed. I had fever, started breaking out, and was very sick. My doctor was out for the holiday. By Tuesday of the next week, I called Faye. I was too ill to drive myself to the hospital. My face on one side was covered in blisters, up into my hair, my mouth was so sore, I could not wear my dentures, my ear was swollen shut. This was on the left side of my face.

When Lucy (nurse) saw me, she replied "I just about know you have shingles". Dr. Henderson saw me quite soon and sent me directly to the hospital. I took 4 different anti-bodies at a time, was there for a week.

After being dismissed, going back next week to Dr. Henderson, my face hurt me so bad. I can't explain this hurt, unless you've had shingles, you would not know. Dr. Henderson said to me "Sometimes people continue to hurt all their lifetime." This was on a Wednesday night. I went back to church with the intention of God healing me. I told him "I can't stand this, and I know you can heal me." He did that very night! Praise the Lord!

__1993__ In 1993, my left hip started hurting me so very badly, I could hardly walk. The first "total hip" had been faithful to me for 18 years. Dr. Jorgenson sent me to the hospital for surgery.

He told me "The hip had jumped out of the socket completely." This time, however, was to be a lot worse surgery than the first "total hip". In the first place, he had to remove the old hip. He had to make another incision to remove bone for the purpose of grafting in the hip. He put another "total hip" on August 8, 1993. I spent 3 weeks in the hospital, but one week was on therapy, I hated that place. Actually, the therapy wasn't too bad, very painful, but the routine they followed wasn't to my liking, but it was probably necessary.

I could not lift my left leg off the bed for a week or more after coming home. I still had the therapy at home for a month or more. Home health lady, plus the one who came to help me get a bath, came for 2 months. Such a blessing.

EMERGENCY ROOM VISITS

<u>1977</u> Once when I lived at the farm, I became very ill with the flu. I came to the emergency room. My doctor gave me medications and I went back home. About 1977.

<u>1992</u> I mentioned going to the emergency room for terrific pain in my shoulder. 2:00 a.m. This was in 1992.

<u>1992</u> This same day, in the late afternoon, I returned to emergency for another injection in my shoulder.

<u>1995</u> On Saturday evening, about 5:30, I had just completed a Bible cover for Andy. This is Grace's baby. I got up off my hospital bed, where I had been sitting, finishing the handwork on it. As I got up, I stumbled over my foot stool which was beside my bed. I had my scissors, the little Bible cover, and the scraps I had left in my hand. When I saw I was falling, I grabbed ahold of my floor lamp, pulling it over, almost pulling my radio off. I fell on the end table, hurting my bad hip, only this is just a flesh wound, one knee on the stool, the other on the floor. I managed to get up, thanking the Lord that I hadn't broken any bones. Then I looked and blood was pouring from my thumb. There lay my scissors. I can't imagine how they became open and cut my left thumb quite badly.

I did not panic. I pressed the quilted scrap of material over the cut, went into the bathroom and put a Band-Aid on. The first one would not stick because of bleeding. I again put a cloth on it and pressure, then I applied another Band-Aid really tight. The blood was coming out, so I put the second one on very tight. I called Elsie. She came for me and took me to emergency, got there about 6:00 pm staying

173

until 12:00 pm. Got some stitches inside and out. What a blessing for a sister nearby. I also got some sore places from the fall. This was March 25, 1995.

CHILDREN OF CECIL AND HAZEL PINKSTON

CHARLES AND LANELLE PINKSTON

CHARLES ROBERT PINKSTON

Charles, you have followed in your dad's footsteps concerning trucking and working so very hard. I am thankful for you, appreciate all you've done thru these last 28 years for me and all the family.

You've been a standby for so many people and God knows and cares. I know he'll reward you. I am thankful you are going to church with your family. You are the mainstay.

Please encourage yourself in the Lord and I believe that things are soon going to be more pleasant for you. I mean I want you to enjoy life some years to come, but you are going to need some rest along the way.

LANELLE MCLAIN PINKSTON

I am thankful to have you for a daughter. You are a good mother, wife, now grandmother, to your household. It's not an easy task to know the way to go, many times when raising a family. We never can know all the answers but when the Lord is our captain, we can depend on him.

I appreciate you helping Charles with his work. I know that I don't know the half of what all you've done, but that's what makes a marriage, is working together. Not necessarily side by side, but in heart.

I thank you for all the nice things you've done for me, and gifts given to me, these last 28 years, which has made my life easier to bear. You've been a person with great faith all your life, in my opinion.

Charles and LaNelle were married June 4, 1956, at Sister Minton's church on Douglas Hi-way, in Nacogdoches, Tx, Nacogdoches County.

BOBBY AND MARY PINKSTON LUMAN

MARY LORENE PINKSTON LUMAN

Mary, I love and appreciate you, always have but as we grow older, our priorities change somewhat. I thank you for being steadfast in living for God most all of your married life these 28 years. Also, for being determined to keep your family together.

Thank you for working hard, giving to the Lord's work, and caring for your children, husband, and grandchildren. I'll say to you like I did Charles, "It's getting time to slow up, take some rest, and enjoy life, accept things you can't change, and thank God for the good things He's already done for you."

ROBERT (BOBBY) CURTIS LUMAN

I appreciate you, Bobby, for all the hard, laboring work you've done thru the years. I know you've gone to work many times when you didn't feel like it.

I thank you for all the caring things you've done for me these last 28 years. You have been willing to do anything I've ever asked of you.

I know that you love Mary and your children, Carla, Chuck, and Linda, and now your sweet grandchildren. Life still holds some pleasant memories of your past, but I believe there's more good things ahead for you and your family.

Thanks for choosing Mary and thus making you my son.

MIKE AND LINDA DALTON

LINDA FAYE PINKSTON DALTON

Linda, I appreciate you, because you remain the same. I admire your persistence, getting things done. I'm speaking of your ability to organize, pull together, and make things simple, that seemed so hard for me.

I thank you for being a hard worker, pulling yourself up by your bootstraps many times, and pressing forward. I thank you for being so generous to all the family, by gifts of money and love.

All these things point to the way you always were, independent, leave me alone, I want to be by myself, do my own thing, and just be 'me'.

MIKE DALTON

I am grateful to have you as a son. I never cease to marvel at all the nice things you think of to do for me, as well as others in the family. Your goodness even spills out to others. These things do not go unnoticed by man or God.

You are an articulate person, but yet you are a hard worker too. I think you are a good husband to Linda. I appreciate you and her working together for the good of reaching your goals.

Thank you for all the nice gifts you have given to me these last 15 years, and all the things you've done for me to make life easier for me.

I appreciate you keeping your place so very well groomed and looking pretty all the time, like someone lives there who is industrious. You have been a godsend many times, helping Linda cook, wash, clean house and serving. I appreciate this too.

EDWARD AND DEBBIE PINKSTON

EDWARD EARL PINKSTON

Edward, you have been the one of my children that has told me so many times, "Mama, don't worry about the bills. You'll figure it out, you always have." Many times, this was a blessing for you to say this.

I appreciate you for all your hard work, loving and caring and making a living for your family. You, too, need to take a week off for you and your family to enjoy and rest your mind and body. It's important from here on out that you do something for enjoyment, not only for you, but for your children and grandchildren to remember about.

DEBORAH ROBERTS PINKSTON

I am very thankful to have you for a daughter. You have been and continue to be a good mother to your children, a good wife, now a loving grandmother.

You have been a blessing to me in many ways. You stayed home when your children were small, which was commendable of you. I certainly believe that you have always been a chaste, pure, virtuous woman.

I appreciate all the nice things you've done for me these last 25 years. Also, all the nice gifts you've picked out and given me for Christmas.

You've been a good help mate for Edward all thru your marriage, like working with him with the crafts and in that shop. Also, you've both enjoyed your yard work and made them so beautiful.

MEMO TO MY CHILDREN

My love for you does not depend

It has not, since you were born

On whether my views you defend,

Adapt, dismiss, or scorn.

So, when your thoughts and mine oppose,

My wish, all else above,

Is that my understanding grows

In measure with my love.

Copied, Author unknown

The wise man looked at him and smiles

No matter how you try…

There are such things like happiness,

That money cannot buy.

True happiness can only come,

From doing good for others.

From treating men everywhere,

As if they were your brothers.

And all the gold in all the world

Could never buy a part…

Of the great happiness you'll know,

When love is in the heart.

Copied, Author unknown

MARK'S TRAGEDY

Charles and LaNelle brought their children, Mark and Grace, to Mississippi to live about three or four years after I had moved there. I was so happy to have all my family together again, but little was I to know that a tragedy was looming up ahead.

I was living in a trailor house on that big high hill. Charles, LaNelle and children were there at my house that afternoon for a little while, but they were on their way home. I believe I left a few minutes ahead of them. I was going down the hi-way to help this girl that had a new baby, the best I remember. She had lived with me awhile. Her husband had been in the service.

Mark was just a little over two years of age, about March of 1969, I'll guess. He really wanted to go with me, but I didn't think I could take him.

When I got back from the girl's house, I decided to go by Mary and Bobby's. When I went to the door and knocked, Mary was on the phone. Finally, she came to the door and asked me, "Have you talked to anyone?" I said, "No." She said, "Mother, Mark has been hit by a pick-up."

Mary's neighbor, Brother Cooper, lived near her and he came out of the house with his shoes in his hands and jumped in a car, I don't know now if it was my car, Mary and Bobby's car, or his car. He drove us to Baptist Hospital on State Street.

They were preparing Mark for surgery. Some of the family and church family had gone in the room to see him, but I would not go. They didn't think he'd live through surgery.

After surgery, the doctors talked to us and told us how bad he was, but if his brain didn't start swelling due to infections or high fever, he could live. They said, "He'll never be able to talk though, because that's the part of his brain he has lost." They explained that they had built his brain up by putting layers of fine silk in it.

Charles and LaNelle wanted me to go into ICU and see him. I didn't want to go. This was probably 1:00 or 2:00 nighttime by then. I finally went to please them. He looked awful. I don't remember if I went home that night or slept in my car.

Incidentally, that night LaVerne, my sister, had a dream about me, seeing me in terrible distress. Believe me, I was, as well as all the family.

I was working, I can't recall how I managed because I was the only one who done my job. Some of us in the family stayed at the hospital day and night all the time.

Mark started having high fever, perhaps some seizures because of fever. They packed his naked body in ice to get the fever down. There were many times we were not allowed to go in and see him at the visiting periods because he was so bad. We had made friends with other people there who had loved ones in ICU. So, they would look over and check on Mark, come out and tell us that there were lots of doctors around his bed or whatever news they could glean.

One day, a man came out and said to us, "I don't see how you folks can stand this." LaNelle looked this man straight in the eye and said to him, "We could not stand it, but you see, we believe he's going to be all right." I told her that day, "It's not by my faith." LaNelle was the strong one then.

Mark became allergic to the strong medications they'd given him so that he began to break out just with a rash at first, then small blisters, then large blisters all over his body. This was when they began packing him in ice.

Six weeks to the day he'd been in ICU, the nurse came out. I was in the waiting room. Charles and LaNelle had gone to the cafeteria. The nurse asked me where the parents were. I told her. Then she told me, "Mark has just shed some real tears like he's coming around." We had carried many things in there trying to get him to notice. It was not long until they moved him to a room.

All during this time, I prayed, "God, let his mind be alright or go ahead and take him." I didn't mean to be cruel, but I didn't think I could handle that. Linda Faye went and bought Mark some new pajamas and came into his room. She said, "Mark, Aunt Linda bought you some new pajamas." He could not get up, but he started trying to get that hospital gown off. I think we all shed tears. I know I did. He continued to get better, but we had lots more trips back to the hospital after getting out. My air conditioner was not working, and it was pretty hot, at least for him. Charles had to take him back just a day or two after we were home.

They did not tell us that he was blind in his left eye at this time. He was under treatment probably two years. He had brain surgery again up there for the stoppage of the spinal fluid. It didn't stop it, though.

When Charles carried him to the eye specialist, he told Charles, "If I had only seen him the next day. The damage was done, unrepairable." Mark had already learned to walk again, even got up and down steps, but this was a real hard blow for Charles and LaNelle.

I believe the doctors in Jackson, Mississippi were Dr. Charles Neil and Dr. Walter Neil. They were brothers. They were very well-known brain surgeons. They had performed surgery all over the world. God was surely with them as well as Mark.

Later, after Mark was twelve years of age, Charles lived at Haltom City. Mark got ill from the spinal fluid leaking out his nose. You see, where that fluid came out, infection could enter. The doctors there at Fort Worth were very skeptical about doing the surgery since the Dr. Neil's had failed to stop the fluid. They were acquainted with them and their work.

Mark had pretty, blond hair. They shaved his head and brought LaNelle his hair. He was in that operation, I believe, 8 or 9 hours.

They cut his scalp from ear to ear. This surgery they did with him sitting straight up.

You see, one of the most frightening things about this was, they could not give him any antibiotics because of him becoming allergic to all of them. They said, "If he just doesn't have any infection, he'll be fine." We'd been told that before but this time he did not have any infection. God was so good to us.

MY PENTECOSTAL HERITAGE

The first Pentecostal preacher I ever heard was Bro. Wesley Mott. He was a fire ball. He had only one leg; he wore an artificial leg. Brother Mott came to Jamesville about 1933.

They built a brush arbor with sawdust floors. Benches were of planks put across blocks to sit on. They used kerosene lanterns for lighting. This top, if built properly, would keep off drizzly rain.

People walked or rode on horseback. Families came in wagons and children often times were put to sleep in their wagons.

This doctrine was new, preached straight to the point, hell and brimstone or Heaven, Jesus, and streets of gold. Not long after Brother Wesley Mott, Brother Bud Luman had received the Holy Ghost and began preaching this same message.

People came from far and near, just to see what was going on. This was the talk in every home in our community because people who believed were receiving the Holy Ghost.

You could hear people praying in their homes long before you got there. I remember one day Mom sent me to Grandma Lee's for something. I heard the praying a long way off. I was reverent of the Lord and their praying, at this age of about 8. I waited quite a while, did not interrupt their praying. They were sitting on the floor, in the fireplace room, in a big circle.

Many of my relatives received the Holy Ghost at this time of revival meeting; Grandma Lee, Aunt Dollie, I believe Aunt Ella but am not sure. The people who lived across the field from us were named Vails. These girls, all 3, received the Holy Ghost. One of them is still living but has been in the hospital recently. This is Sister Frances Vail Rogers. Sister Brooksie Holt Fitzgerald was another person who comes to mind.

It was about this time that we children started playing church on the back porch. We had preaching, praying, singing, and shouting. In other words, the beginning of my being God conscious. Concerned about my soul, learning to pray, and expecting an answer.

I recollect the road being full of people going to church revival, walking for 3 miles each way with their children, and they got to church on time.

Later they had prayer meetings in the homes. If a preacher was available, they came and preached. People were humble and tired of their religion; thus, they were blessed to receive the Holy Ghost and afterwards they enjoyed their salvation by worship and praise.

Many dear old saints suffered much heartache and great persecutions for going to church. Their husbands would lay beside the road and wait for their return to abuse them. I know some men who hid in the loft of their home with a shotgun and threatened the family. You see, God was moving, and the Devil was also.

My mother-in-law received the Holy Ghost during the early preaching of the truth. Many of my father-in-law's sisters embraced the Holy Ghost: Aunt Fannie Flowers, Aunt Gladys Husband, and Uncle Gus Husband. I mention Brother Bud Luman, Sister Lonie Luman, Sister Carrie Minton, Sister Rosella Owens, Sis. Donahoe, and Sister Mildred Pate (I loved her dearly.).

I heard Sis. Lonie Luman which was Brother Bud Luman's wife say, "Bud was the meanest man she ever saw before he received the Holy Ghost."

Everyone who lived in 'No Man's Land', this is what is called the 'Glory Land' community now, knew Bud Luman. He was a bad man in the community. Also, he stole from people all over. I guess this was true. My father-in-law said, "After Bud Luman received the Holy Ghost, he gathered up wagon loads of plow tools and returned them to their rightful owners." Brother Bud was really a man of God after his conversion. He trusted God for everything, including his healing. He died trusting the Lord. He died in the parsonage of Sister Minton's church on the Douglas highway.

This was Bobby Luman's granddaddy.

I've heard Brother Wiley Holland tell how he trusted God as a young man for his $1.00 for offering each service. God always provided it.

I know these old people must have prayed for their children and grandchildren. I'm thankful that I had a Grandmother Lee with the Holy Ghost long ago.

The traveling preachers stayed in the homes when they held revivals. They didn't get much money. They got syrup, eggs, corn, or whatever people had to give. Many times, they preached when they were hungry. Sometimes, people in the homes mistreated the preachers badly.

People long ago worked hard, no conveniences, not many cars, yet were more organized than people today. We should be ashamed. These people were paving the way for us each and every meeting they had.

Most of us are always in a fever to 'do something' for God, but we are missing the point. The first thing that God wants, is for us to 'be something' for him.

I started to read my Bible and at the scripture where it said in Joshua 24:15 "Choose you this day whom you will serve." I thought that meant what it said (that day) and I better be making a decision for myself, and I did.

I didn't have to suffer as many things that people back then had to suffer when I received the Holy Ghost. There was quite a bit of opposition, even so. There were no Pentecostal churches nearby, just prayer meetings in the homes. I went when I could, prayed an awful lot, read my Bible every possible minute I could. These things were to be a foundation for my life.

I was baptized in 1940, I believe, and received the Holy Ghost about that time. Sister Mildred Pate was one of sisters who really prayed with me and for me. I did not have a church to attend regularly until after I married which was in 1944. Since then, I have tried to be faithful to my church, pastor, and support of the church thru tithes and offerings and any need that arose.

COVE SPRINGS REUNION

Each year they had a Cove Springs Reunion. People came from far and near. They spread lunch on the ground by spreading sheets out and putting all the food on it. Oftentimes several families would spread their food together.

The year the triplet babies were born, there were so many people there that they parked their cars for a mile or more, really close to our home. I have a clipping in the picture section concerning this particular year. It was estimated that from 3000 to 6000 people attended the year of 1928, which I remember distinctly. We only lived about one mile away.

When my dad was a child, they were at Cove Springs at church, and they left Dad asleep on the church pew. They went all the way home before missing him and had to return to fetch him.

Someone sold that church building and moved it away about 1986 or 1987. Everyone was very unhappy about it. The pews had brass plaques on the backside, with the name of the person who paid for that pew. My Dad's name, Robert D. Lee, was one of them.

HALTOM WRITES ABOUT OLD TIME CAMP MEETINGS

In Giles Haltom's 1928 anniversary edition of the Daily Sentinel, he wrote a story about camp meetings at Cove Springs and at Simpson's campground at Melrose.

He wrote that on February 17, 1858, Daniel H. Vail, in order to help in the cause of his Divine Master, deeded 30 acres of land on which the famous spring (Cove Spring) was located.

Mr. Giles Haltom mentioned all the trustees by name, also they were changed from time to time. I want to attempt to name them here. A church was to be built for school and church purposes. The church was built to satisfy the directive of the deed, but primarily for use of camp meetings.

This church was moved a few years ago, without permission was my understanding.

On October 9, 1927, a remarkable gathering of people took place at old Cove Spring campground. I remember all the cars and people passing our house. We only lived about a mile away.

This was a reunion of old timers, who had formerly gone there and camped in small houses made for the purpose. This article said that about 45 of these small houses were built. They had dirt floors, but they made frames to put their mattresses on. This was before my time.

There was an arbor there at the same time also. It was estimated that between 3000 to 6000 people attended this year in 1927.

People came from Nacogdoches, Shelby, and San Augustine counties. This was what prompted the building of the big brush arbor, because the church house was too small.

186

In order to have sufficient light available for night services at the big arbor, small scaffolds, four feet in height and covered with dirt, were built, a half dozen on each side of the arbor, and a man of color was employed to keep pine knots on these scaffolds during the services.

Sometimes these meetings lasted 2 weeks.

One of the interesting features of the old-time camp meetings that will not be forgotten by many people now living was the part played by Charlie Byrd, a well-known man of color of that day. (I really don't know when this article was printed, but I don't think it's been that long.) This man obtained an acre or two of land near the spring and installed several 'sheds' or 'shanties' of considerable size in which he kept a supply of cold drinks, cakes, pies, barbecued meats, in fact, a restaurant, where people might get a good meal if they so desired. He also had a corral of considerable size arranged, large enough to hold a considerable number of horses, with many long and short troughs for feeding purposes.

Charlie Byrd kept a sufficient quantity of corn and fodder on hand to feed many horses. It was a great help for this man's foresight to provide these things, which were almost a necessity. As long as he conducted his business at Cove Springs during the camp meeting, there was no disorderly conduct around his place, but on the contrary, everything was done decently and in order.

This article gave the names of presiding elders and preachers who served the church on the Melrose circuit since the year of 1873. I went through these names and am giving some names that I am familiar with:

Frank Stovall, J.W. Johnson, Jesse Lee (my dad's brother), A.J. Weeks, John Windham, W.L. Pate, John Heppenstell, Charles McKnight, I.F. Pace, W.W. Hooper, Ed J. Harris

A TRIBUTE TO MY PASTOR, BRO. WILLOUGHBY

I thank my Lord and Savior for a pastor that is knowledgeable, kind, and understanding with his flock.

It amazes me that when, at my darkest hour, I go to church, and he brings a message directly to me. This gives me new power and refreshes my mind, just knowing God is real, and that I have a pastor who obeys the leading of the spirit.

The things that he gives us from the pulpit, gives us new strength. He has a way of strengthening the things that remain, giving us a new beginning.

It must be so hard at times for a pastor to have to cut down to the root and try to salvage some flicker of good that we still possess. You seem to do this with love and caring.

Then there's courage. You pass encouragement out to us. I believe a great deal of talent is lost in this world for the want of a little courage, thank you for understanding this.

I've spoken much about my ancestors and old pioneers. Brother Willoughby, you will be the one these small children will be speaking about years from now. You will be their Pentecostal pioneer.

Every now and then our soul has to be refreshed. We receive this by coming to church and the hearing of the Word. We could lose heart and hope, if we didn't have a pastor like you to bring the wonderful messages to us, thus reviving our souls.

Thank you for reminding me of these facts just recently in one of your messages.

1. "Did I learn, from the trial, what Jesus wanted me to learn, so I won't go thru the same one again?"
2. "When I look back, do I understand how the Lord was developing me for my good?"

3. "No sadder waste than to go through something and not learn."

You have helped me to believe that no experience need pass without leaving me a gift. Helping me, I hope, to grow in the Lord, making me a better person, and more giving to others.

So, when you are tired and weary, just remember what it means for us to hear you break the Bread of Life to us. I pray the Lord encourages you, gives you strength, and good health.

May the Lord ever bless your ministry and your family.

THE IMPORTANCE OF A NAME

I am thankful for my heritage. From my mom's side which was Hooper, Hinkle, and McGraw's and from my dad's side which was Lee, Byrd, Cole, and Batton's. I have studied quite extensively recently about my heritage.

After reading from available material, I've been made to realize how very much we should appreciate our 'name'. You know, we are all proud of our name. Our name is important. Even just to hear someone call our name means so much to that particular individual.

The Bible tells us in Ecclesiastes 7:1 "A good name is better than precious ointment; and the day of death than the day of one's birth".

Proverbs 22:1 tells us "A good name is to be chosen rather than great riches, loving favor rather than silver and gold."

Our parents, grandparents, and great grandparents were proud of their name, which was an honorable one. Among our people, some were political, religious, and educated. Our older generations had to fight perhaps not so much in wars, but in everyday warfare of famine, Indians, heat, cold, hunger, and deaths. Yet, in spite of all these hardships, they had the courage and, I'm sure, faith in God to keep them keeping on. We have every reason to be thankful and grateful for our names.

FOR MY BABIES AND PRE-SCHOOL CHILDREN

A good name does not come easy. We kind of have to earn it. I'll try to explain this, according as I see it. We start learning on our moms' knees or sitting at her feet. We also start learning from our dads by age six months. At first our abilities aren't much, but we learn to know our parents, love their attention and doing the pretty little things they ask of us. A few years and Mom and Dad start telling us, "Children, honor your father and mother." "Mind me." "Play pretty together." "Listen to me." They start telling you that Jesus loves you and the Bible tells us to be obedient. This is learning obedience.

When Mom or Dad tell you children; put up your toys, hang up your clothes, take out the trash, clean up your room, they are giving you great teaching. The Bible says, "Obedience is better than sacrifice."

The word sacrifice means to give up something that you have and would love to keep, but you give it to someone else. This is sacrificing, but to obey is better than sacrifice. We are speaking of what constitutes the making of a good name.

YOUTH

Reading your Bible every day tells you and me how to live. We all know, most all of us are old enough to read, that the Bible tells us we are all going to die someday. So, it doesn't hurt to think about it and our accountability to God. An honest, dependable, industrious person is always wanted. They will be respected and loved. They will be spoken of in words of high commendation.

These traits are good for both girls and boys and will make either one to grow up to be a man or woman of known worth and established character. We have to start from childhood to make an honorable name for ourselves.

I have read books about afflicted children, one recently where the little boy had cerebral palsy. His wish was for two things: to be normal, the other to be a preacher. Even though both looked impossible, with God, parents, and his determination, he mastered both desires. I will say he made a Pentecostal pastor at that.

YOUNG AND OLDER

I am thankful that none of my family are lazy. This being one trait I deplore. I believe any parents that don't begin to teach their children to work around the house when small, will regret it.

We can love our children and still expect them to get out and start working, even before they finish school. In fact, this is the best time to get a part-time job. We learn a lesson from the eagles. They stir up their nests when the eaglets are hardly able to fly.

Everyone should remember that each step they take toward the goal of wealth or honor gives them increased energy, power, and happiness. Never, never think what you do for someone else is time, money, or energy misspent.

The building of our good name depends on many things, many sleepless nights many hard-working days, lots of prayers, and many failures. As long as we are trying and making mistakes, there is hope. Our own errors may often teach us more than the precepts of others. Believe me, I speak from experience. It's more important to not compare ourselves to others.

A man was made to protect, love, and cherish, not to under value, neglect, or abuse women.

If someone speaks evil of you, let your life be such that none will believe him.

Always live, misfortune excepted, within your income. Never borrow money if you can avoid it. But if needs be, to have lasting friends, go to a bank to borrow, that's their business.

Good character is above all else. Your character cannot be essentially injured except by your own acts. Try never to speak evil of anyone. I remember old Brother Brown saying 40 years ago, "When you speak something about someone, even if it's truth, you immediately put the damper on your spirit."

Keep good company or none at all. I remember when Hershel got in trouble. He was with a bunch of boys and the boys wanted to steal a truck from Sutton's sawmill. He didn't want to partake of the stealing, but he got in the back and rode off with them. They all got caught and put in jail. I recall someone coming to the farm, where Dad was working, and told him. He left and went to Nacogdoches to get him out of jail. My, how I prayed. You would have thought he was on his way to prison, the way I prayed.

Never be idle, if not with your hands, attend to the cultivation of your mind. Speak the truth and you won't to have to remember to whom or what you told the last time.

I hate to make promises, afraid I'll forget, so I don't make many promises, but if I do, I fulfill my engagements, even if I do have to make notes.

Keep your own secrets if you have any. God is the one who knows, and he cares, no one else does.

Don't tell people outside of family of your aches, pains, troubles, and heartaches. They may ask but they don't really want to know especially when I get through telling all about my aches and pains. I need prayer on this.

THE MOST IMPORTANT NAME

I have attempted to name things that surely will make each of us an honorable name. A good name here on Earth is important but we must meet the requirements to make it into heaven and to do that we must have the Name of Jesus applied to us in water baptism and be filled with the Holy Ghost.

There's lots of hallowed things we could mention, but the name of Jesus is the most wonderful name we could ever call on or mention.

Philippians 2: 9-11 "Wherefore God also hath highly exalted him and given him a name which is above every name: That at the name of Jesus every knee should bow, of things in heaven, and things in earth, and things under the earth; And that every tongue should confess that Jesus Christ is Lord, to the glory of God the Father."

If God gave him a name that is above every name, then the name of Jesus would be above the name of Jehovah. The name Jesus is the Greek equivalent of the Hebrew Jehoshua, which is Jehovah Savior or one of the compound names of God such as Jehovah Rapha: the Lord Who Heals, Jehovah Shalom: The Lord is Peace, Jehovah Nissi: The Lord my Refuge or Jehovah Jireh: The Lord will Provide.

Any name that would be the greatest would have to belong to the Almighty God.

The Almighty God's name is Jesus.

John 5:43 tells us, "I am come in my Father's name, and ye receive me not: If another shall come in his own name, him ye will receive."

John 10: 25-26 "Jesus answered them, I told you, and ye believed not: the works that I do in my Father's name, they bear witness of me. But ye believe not, because ye are not of my sheep, as I said unto you."

The Son's Name is Jesus.

Matthew 1:21 "And she shall bring forth a son, and thou shalt call his name Jesus: for he shall save his people from their sins."

The Holy Ghost's Name is Jesus.

John 14:26 "But the Comforter, which is the Holy Ghost, whom the Father will send in my name, he shall teach you all things, and bring all things to your remembrance, whatsoever I have said unto you."

Matthew 28:19 "Go ye therefore, and teach all nations, baptizing them in the name of the Father, and of the Son, and of the Holy Ghost:"

This scripture did not open up the disciples understanding as he did in Luke 24:45-47 "Then opened he their understanding, that they might understand the scriptures, And said unto them, Thus it is written, and thus it behooved Christ to suffer, and to rise from the dead the third day: And that repentance and remission of sins should be preached in his name among all nations, beginning at Jerusalem."

Peter, full of the Holy Ghost, preached Acts 2:38 "Then Peter said unto them, Repent, and be baptized every one of you in the name of Jesus Christ for the remission of sins, and ye shall receive the gift of the Holy Ghost."

There's repentance and remission of sins in Jesus Name. Where did this begin? It began at Jerusalem. That's the fulfillment of Luke 24:47.

Father, Son, and Holy Ghost spoken of in Matthew 28:19 are titles. Just for instance, you take a man; he's a father and a son but these are not his name. They are only titles. So, we are to use the name of the titles in Matthew 28:19, which is Jesus.

Acts 10:48 "And he commanded them to be baptized in the name of the Lord. Then prayed they him to tarry certain days."

Paul preached it in Acts 19:5 "When they heard this, they were baptized in the name of the Lord Jesus."

Colossians 3:17 "And whatsoever ye do in word or deed, do all in the name of the Lord Jesus, giving thanks to God and the Father by him."

Some additional scriptures where it says to baptize in the name of Jesus.

Acts 8:16, Acts 10:48

Ephesians 4:5 "One Lord, one faith, one baptism."

I know a lady who read in her Bible where it said to be baptized in the name of the Father, the Son, the Holy Ghost. Her grandson was a college student at S.F.A. He lived with her. When he came in that night, she showed him the verse Matthew 28:19. He told her, "Well, I'd first find out what the name is." She replied, "Bless God, I know what the Name is, it's Jesus!" So, she had her grandson to take her to a church to be baptized in Jesus Name that night. She already had the Holy Ghost.

John 3:5 "Jesus answered, Verily, verily, I say unto thee, except a man be born of water and of the Spirit, he cannot enter into the kingdom of God."

I Corinthians 6:19 "What? know ye not that your body is the temple of the Holy Ghost which is in you, which ye have of God, and ye are not your own?"

I trust these good scriptures will be helpful to some of you and if we live accordingly, we will be worthy to bear His Name. We as Christians have an awesome responsibility to live a life pleasing to Jesus. We cannot do things, I should say we don't have a desire to do things, as we once did. Jesus in us, the hope of glory, makes the difference.

Going to church is a necessity because our strength comes from others and hearing the Word of the Lord.

Let us forever strive to have an honorable name which our forefathers would be pleased with and, more importantly, our Father in Heaven.

There are so many privileges that Jesus Name gives us access to here on Earth. Just to mention a few: Power, Healing, Forgiveness, Trust, and Faith. Most of all, we have a promise of going to Heaven.

PLEASURES OF LIFE

If someone asked me what I enjoyed more than anything, I would say, "First and foremost, My Lord and Savior Jesus Christ." Just knowing he saved me, it gives me much pleasure to live for him.

I love to go to church, to praise and worship the Lord. To hear the Word of the Lord gives me what I need so many times and when I need it the most. Can you imagine a God like that? Oh, I know many believe this.

My own immediate family has given me much happiness, although there's been many sleepless nights and heartaches, but considering my oldest child being 50 years of age and also the fact that I have 34 in my family, my worries certainly could have been more, so I thank God for my family.

Then my sisters and brothers have been a blessing to me so many times. I love all of them more than words can say.

I have so many nieces and nephews that I'll just say I love you all and pray for all of you. My brother and sisters-in-law are all outstanding in my eyes. They've been a blessing to me.

I love and appreciate my present pastor, Brother W.E. Willoughby, and his wife, Sister Willoughby. My church family means more than I can put into words. I appreciate every one of my brothers and sisters in the Lord.

I get pleasure from working for the furtherance of the gospel. Just to help anyone go to the mission field or anyone in need gives me pleasure.

My grandchildren have brought me much pleasure in life. When they were small, I got to go see them or they came to see me. Now they have families and have to work. Now I can enjoy my sweet, sweet great grandchildren if I could just see them and be with them more often, I'd be much, much, much happier.

My greatest pleasure and desire at the ending of my way will be a comfort for me to trust I've had some good influence upon others. One big question we all need to ask is what we are leaving behind us, in the lives of others. We all have influence. Is it good or bad? We are just passing on as we travel through life. The real test is how have we handled our heartaches and disappointments. None of us know what we may have to face. The future is uncertain. The Psalmist David wrote in Psalms 23:6 "Surely goodness and mercy shall follow me all the days of my life." This can only be accomplished through Jesus.

EPILOGUE

WORDS FROM THE CHILDREN

MAMA'S FINAL YEARS

By Linda Pinkston Dalton

After living in Mississippi for almost ten years, Mama returned home to Texas. She lived at the farm, south of Chireno. At first, she lived by herself in her mobile home, which was parked by the "little red" house just down the road from Ma and Pa Lee's house. During this time, Mama worked some at a mom-and-pop country store and also sold Home Interior. She attended Gloryland Pentecostal Church in San Augustine County and was always an active member. Brother Freeman Bryant was her pastor.

After her twin brother died, Mama and Ma Lee moved to Nacogdoches. Mama was so glad to be back in town. They both attended Greater Faith Tabernacle Church on South St, or Old Lufkin Highway, as it's now called. Her pastor there was Brother William Willoughby. She worked tirelessly for her church for many years.

Mama had the opportunity to work with Mary and me on the first research project we did back in the early 90s. She was so excited to be earning a paycheck. We had only been back home a few days and she was lonesome. We planned to meet at Henderson for her to ride with me to do some work in Anderson County. That morning, it was misty raining. I called her to see if she wanted to stay home because of the weather, but nothing doing, she was coming to meet me. We were gone until mid-afternoon.

On the way back to Henderson, we stopped at a Dairy Queen to get her a blizzard; I'll never forget the big smile on her face coming out of the DQ. I dropped her off at her car and she was supposed to call me as soon as she got home. I was getting a little worried by the time I got home because she hadn't called yet. This was in the early days of cell phones. I waited and waited but no call. I was calling everyone trying to see if something was wrong.

Finally, I received a call from her sister, Aunt Elsie, who told me Mama had been in a bad car wreck, and she was badly hurt. I couldn't get in touch with my sister, my husband, or my brothers. I couldn't leave until Mike got home and since Mary was closer to Nacogdoches than I was, Mary went. When she got to the hospital, all of Mama's sisters and Aunt Lucy was at the hospital in the waiting room. They were all crying and comforting each other, not knowing if Mama would live or not.

This was our worst nightmare. Mama was all but crushed in the wreck. Her left leg and hip, her heart, her neck, and ribs; in fact, there wasn't much in her body that wasn't affected. It was touch and go for days, not knowing if she'd make it or not. She was black and blue all over.

I remember when she finally knew enough to know what happened, she asked me did she get her check that she'd been waiting on from the work she did with us. It had in fact come, but it was months before she even felt like going in a store. After a very long hospital stay and rehab, she was finally able to be dismissed, but it was the beginning of the end for Mama. This was the summer of 1998.

It seemed like my Mama endured more than anyone should have had to endure, but she was always strong, strong in her faith and mind.

Her last few months was spent in nursing homes. Mary and I tried to see her as much as we could during this time. We stayed with her around the clock during her last days on earth. Carla, Mary's oldest daughter, and Grace, Charles and LaNelle's daughter, also took turns sitting up with her. Mary had been there all day the day before she died, so we convinced her to go home and let us stay. Carla and Grace were with me the last night. I brought handwork for us to do, and the girls embroidered almost all night. Grace and I buried ours with Mama and Carla wanted to keep hers as a reminder of her Granny.

We knew the time was close; Charles was trying to get home from a work trip and Edward had planned to come back that morning. We kept trying to call Mary; somehow her phone had gotten turned off, but we finally reached her, and she made it to the nursing home in time. After Mary got there, I stepped out in the hall and the winner of American Idol (the night before), was singing "Flying without Wings".

There were several of us there when Mama passed. Carla and Lynda were singing "When Jesus Passed By" when she left this world. After a few minutes, Carla walked out in the hall, and she said there was a hush in that nursing home like they'd never seen before. It is impossible to write in words what we all felt in that room as angels came to take Mama home.

A few days prior to mama's passing, Brother Willoughby came to the hospital to see her. We talked about the funeral plans, and I mentioned that I wanted her funeral to be a celebration of Mama's life, rather than a sermon. I told him her biggest regret in life was not graduating from school. Brother Willoughby had been a professor at SFA; for the funeral, he donned cap and gown and had a 'graduation' service for Mama.

Hazel Iva Lee Pinkston, July 19, 1925 – May 27, 2003, graduated with honors! She was 77 years of age.

Mama was buried beside our beloved father at the Upper Chireno Cemetery in Nacogdoches County, Texas.

OUR MEMORIES

MEMORIES BY CHARLES ROBERT PINKSTON

A child could not ask for a better town to grow up in than Nacogdoches, Texas, especially when you had a hardworking, loving family who loved God. Such was the Pinkston family.

My earliest memory as a child was when my dad bought me a new pair of cowboy boots. I can't tell you my exact age, but it was between 3-5. We were at Pa Lee's farm and there had been a heavy rain. I was walking in the garden and walked right out of the new muddy boots. They were found a couple of weeks later. I never remember my dad getting on to me for ruining those boots.

Our mother was the hardest working lady I ever knew. She made all our shirts up until I was in the 7th grade and probably some after then. She was an amazing cook, and we never went to bed hungry. Dad was a pretty fair cook as well. They could both stir up a meal out of something.

We loved animals but never let them stay in the house. One evening, we were all at the kitchen table eating. The front door was open, and a neighbor's cat just walked in and went under the table. I saw it and my father also saw it. Neither of us said a word! Mother always wore a long dress. The cat moved in between her legs and curled its tail around one of them. Mother's eyes froze and her eyes got really big. She grabbed that table and turned it upside down! Food, poly pop, and dishes flying, people screaming, chaos everywhere! My dad never said a word and the cat ran out the door, never to return! I think Mother thought it was a snake!

One summer, our first cousins from Pennsylvania came to visit. We were in Pinky Pa's field and the older girl, Sandy, asked what kind of flower that was. Right away, (and I am ashamed of this), I told her it was the state flower of Texas and she had to rub it for good luck. It was a bull nettle bush. When she rubbed it, she immediately started crying and I was laughing. When we got home, I wasn't laughing. My mother gave me a switching I never forgot. Mother believed "spare the rod, spoil the child". I got my fair share of switching and am equally sure I deserved every one of them. They made me a better man.

Growing up was so much different in those days. Edward and I would leave on Saturday morning and explore East Texas all day. We would try to be home by supper time. We were not afraid, and it was just something to do.

When I was about 6 or 7 years old, Mother carried me to the barber shop and told me to get a close haircut. There were several customers ahead of me, and when it came my turn, I forgot what Mother said, so I told them she wanted me to get a SLOW haircut. When I finally got through, Mother had left. (Women did not go in barber shops.) I walked home. I walked about 2 ¼ miles to school every day until Mother got her license in about 1953. Walking about 2 ½ miles to go home from the barber shop was no big deal.

In 1959, Dad rented a house in San Augustine County for the summer so he could be close to the river to fish and hunt. He was a great outdoorsman. One hot day, we were washing that new car behind the house with 5-gallon buckets of well water. We were all soaking wet, so I didn't see any harm in throwing that 5-gallon bucket of soapy water on my dad. I guess it was a little colder than I figured. He had a wet mop in his hand and hit me beside my head with it. We were all laughing and having fun.

My little sister, Linda, wanted a piano but couldn't play. My mother told her if she would learn to play one, she would get her a piano. One year later, Linda was playing for our church. Mother, somehow, managed to find one.

There are so many fond memories of my childhood. I could tell you so many stories about each of us kids. Like Mary having 3 dates the same night. I can't remember just how that turned out.

I bought a '48 Ford pickup that was bright red with spinner hubcaps and a bone steering wheel. The truck had a blown head gasket when I sold it. Edward was just learning to drive, and he really wanted that truck but was not old enough for it.

Skipping Sunday School was not an option at our home. Mother insisted we go no matter what. One Sunday, it was pouring down rain. I had a '46 Chevrolet pickup and those had very small cabs. We loaded 7 or possibly 8 teenagers in the seat of that truck. We went to church! It had stopped raining after church so there were 3 in the front and 4 or 5 in the bed of the truck when we went home.

We had a really great childhood with a loving mother and father.

There would be many stories to tell of my childhood. I tried to tell you just a few. You see, one has many more as a young adult, meeting my God given wife, LaNelle, our three children Mark, Grace, and Aaron, a new life as a parent, and many stories of a good life.

We cannot bring back yesterday but we can recall the wonderful memories. So, one must purpose to live today in such a way that tomorrow our family can look back, as we have, with great memories of their own.

MEMORIES BY MARY LORENE PINKSTON LUMAN

My memory of Dad is he was a hardworking man. He loved his family and was always looking for ways to make money. Dad was always traveling wherever he had to buy and sell to make sure his family was provided for. He loved nice clothes and always dressed nice. Of course, Mother made sure his clothes were starched and ironed. When dad started showing signs of health problems, I remember he wasn't able to find work at home so he could provide for his family.

My Mother was my everything growing up. I felt like I was a mama's girl. She was always busy and needed help, so I was right with her to do whatever was to be done. Mother was a good example for us.

She didn't just tell us kids to do things, she let us help her, so we also learned how to do them. She taught me to sew, clean house, do crafts, and cook. Most importantly, she taught all of us to go to church, pray and put God first in our lives. She showed us that you can love people regardless of our differences.

Mother believed if something needed to be done you made a way for it to happen, not to give up when times get hard.

Mother taught us to love each other and not talk bad about our siblings. She was a good example to follow because she loved her brothers and sisters and never talked bad about them. Mother taught us kids not to argue and we didn't.

All of Mother's love and teachings has helped me in raising my children and handling problems with love and compassion.

Today I wish I could tell Mother and Daddy what a beautiful family they have and how their lives formed our bond with each other. I miss them and thank them for their love and teachings.

MEMORIES BY LINDA FAYE PINKSTON DALTON

Mama was probably the most practical person I've ever known. She was multi-talented and could do anything she set her mind to do, including re-modeling our house, which she did many times; she loved to sew, work on crafts, and cook. She was also an excellent teacher and taught Sunday School for many years. She was the hardest working woman I've ever known. She loved books and read thousands in her lifetime. Mama was a caregiver; at times her health was much worse than the one she was caring for. Mama took pride in the way her husband, her children, and her home looked. She believed this was a direct reflection of her and made sure we were well cared for, fed, and clean.

Daddy was an entrepreneur, well ahead of his time. He once built a home on a chassis long before that was common. Daddy was a man's man; if something broke, he fixed it. He tied his own hoop nets, fishing with them and trotlines. He trapped in the winter, whittling his own frames to stretch the hides on. He fished year-round, no matter how cold or hot it was. He raised and sold watermelons and bought many truckloads of anything he could sell, including hay. He was a family man and called his children his babies. Daddy loved to whistle. He was a great cook and helped Mama clean. He loved to stay busy.

Our house was a happy home where many cousins and neighborhood children were always welcome.

When I think of Mama and Daddy, I think of home. I think of Mama in the kitchen cooking while Daddy happily danced around her. I think of Daddy in the back yard, with his net strung in the tree, while he whistled and worked on his net, or Mama sitting under the tree at the side of the house, peeling a truck load of tomatoes Daddy had brought home to be canned.

Home is many things to many people, but to me, it was a safe place. It was a place that will always live in my heart as the happiest times of my life. I miss home.

MEMORIES BY EDWARD EARL PINKSTON

The most important things I learned in life were things I learned from my father, in the short 14 years we had together. I feel he was the best teacher I ever had.

I learned honesty. I learned how to have empathy for people less fortunate than myself. I learned to always be happy and content with what I had.

As for my mom, she was a very fascinating and talented lady. Based on the examples she set, I came to feel I could do anything I wanted to do.

I remember upholstering furniture with her. I remember helping her with carpentry. She helped me believe nothing was impossible, to have initiative, and to be creative. I love her and miss her very much.

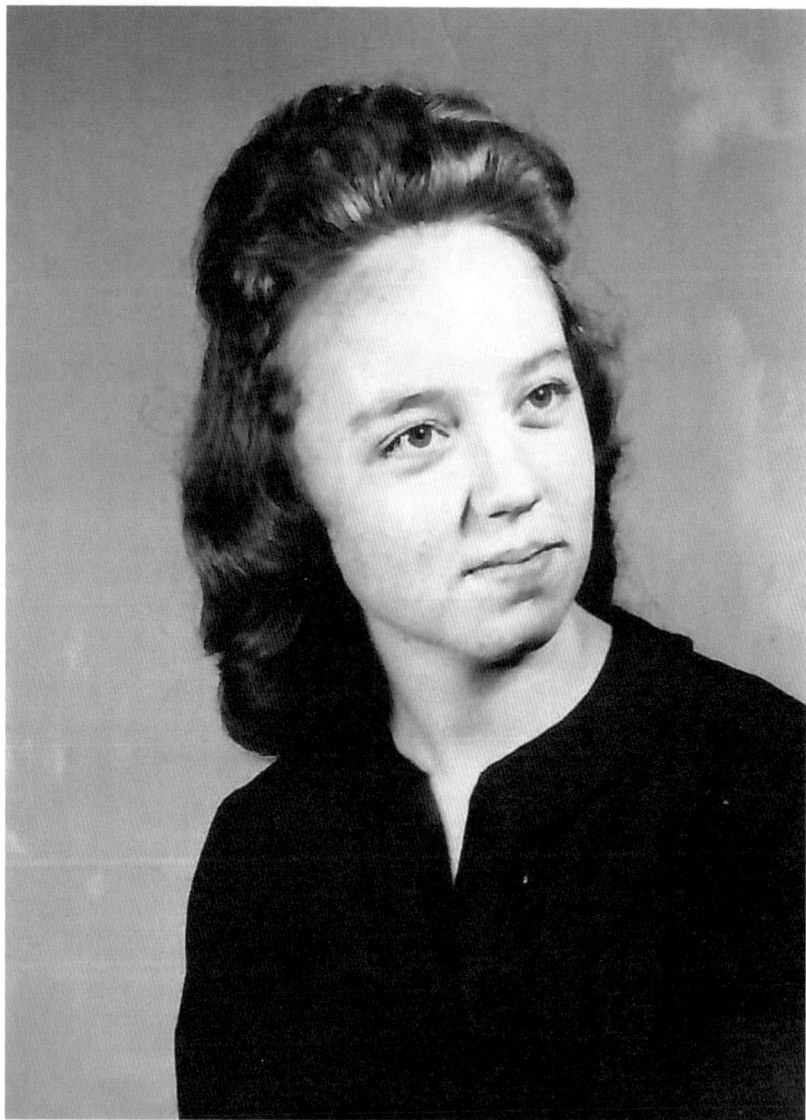

LINDA F. PINKSTON DALTON – AGE 16

MARY L. PINKSTON LUMAN – AGE 17

CHARLES R. PINKSTON

EDWARD E. PINKSTON

EDWARD, MARY, LINDA, HAZEL (MAMA), CHARLES

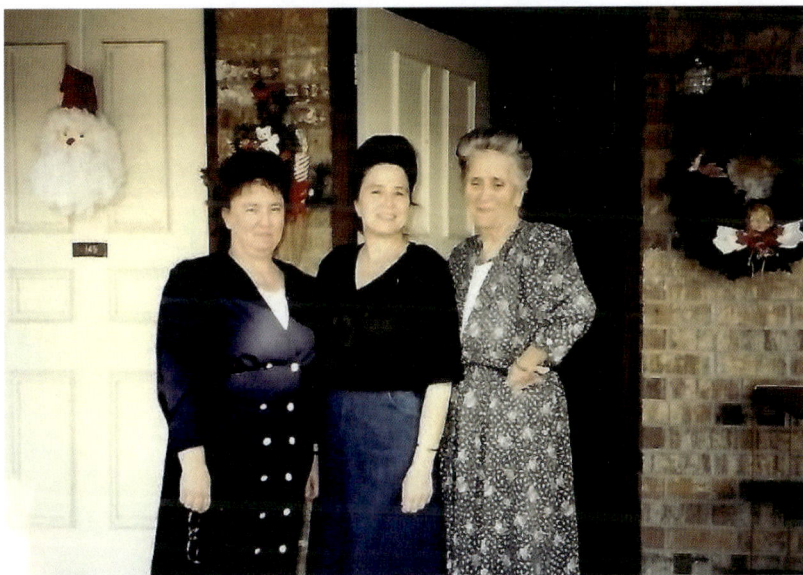

LINDA, MARY, HAZEL LEE PINKSTON (MAMA)

ROBERT D. LEE'S (PA)

DAIRY BARN AT THE FARM

HAZEL LEE PINKSTON (MAMA)

GIVING A PRESENTATION AT CHURCH

MARY PINKSTON LUMAN

&

LINDA PINKSTON DALTON

PINKY MA'S SISTERS IN THE KITCHEN

Thank you for reading Mama's Story. The life our mother lived is at the core of our own life values. Due to the example of our loving parents, we've always strived to find ways to strengthen our family bond.

Pinky Ma's Sisters in the Kitchen was inspired by our mother's love of cooking. We grew up in an era when family came first, and hard times made you closer. We have an incredible bond that we decided to share with the world. We would love to have you share our lives, delicious recipes, and love for people on our Facebook page live cooking videos. Our website contains recipes, cooking videos, online store, and much more.

Facebook: Pinky Ma's Cakes, Cookies & Candy

Website: pinkymaskitchen.com.

YouTube: PinkyMa's Kitchen

Information to order more copies of this book is on the website.